KABBALAH

6/12/91

Diana:

I Hope you enjoy this book, it is one of my favorite Kabbalah.

Lienor

KABBALAH
Your Path to Inner Freedom

Ann Williams-Heller

*This publication is made possible with
the assistance of the Kern Foundation*

Quest Books

The Theosophical Publishing House
Wheaton, Ill. U.S.A.
Madras, India/London, England

The Theosophical Publishing House
306 West Geneva Road
Wheaton, IL 60187

A publication of the Theosophical Publishing House, a department of the Theosophical Society in America.

Library of Congress Cataloging in Publication Data

Williams-Heller, Ann, 1904-1988.
    Kabbalah : your path to inner freedom / Ann Williams-Heller. — 1st ed.
        p.   cm. — (Quest books)
    Includes bibliographical references.
    ISBN 0-8356-0656-2 : $9.95
    1. Cabala.   I. Title.
BF1611.W77 1990
135'.4—dc20   89-40624
                                                           CIP

Printed in the United States of America

This book is dedicated to those
who led me to The Tree of Life,
and to the Good, the Beautiful and
the True
in
You.

Acquaint now thyself with him, and be at peace; thereby good shall come unto thee.
Job 22:21

Contents

Contents

Figures & Tables

Preface

God has been in my life as long as I can remember. I was about four years old when my mother told me, "God sees and hears everything." It frightened me, and left me always with a strange feeling when I did something I knew was wrong. But I was curious as well as scared and wanted to know why I could not see and hear God also. So, I was on the constant lookout and begged Him silently after every goodnight prayer to talk to me. Then one day I figured it out: God was a giant, hiding inside the huge grandfather clock in the children's room in our home in Vienna. There, locked behind the large glass door, his two big fingers moved steadily over his shiny face and his gold ball below sounded "tick-tock" as it swung incessantly from side to side.

As time passed, with beautiful and also difficult years, this childhood search for God remained with me. An insatiable curiosity became a lifelong quest. Then came Walter, my husband. For thirty-three years he filled my life with rare treasures and shared my interest in the unseen God. Together we explored the great religions of the world and some of their later offshoots. In a scholarly fashion we devoted ourselves to the profound thoughts of sages, past and present. This metaphysical pursuit of intense zigzag study—our foremost avocation, a lasting benefit—shaped our mutual goal in life. From Hinduism we journeyed to Northern Buddhism ... from Christianity and the Bible to Islam and the glorious Koran ... from Zoroaster to Hermes Trismegistus ... from the

Egyptian to *The Tibetan Book of the Dead* . . . from
the harmony of pristine Gregorian chants to the music of the spheres in esoteric astrology . . . from the
pearls of Greek and Roman mythology to the Tao, the
I-Ching and the mystery of Zen. We looked into the
ageless numbers of Pythagoras, the royal road of Gautama the Buddha, the eternal freedom of Socrates,
the sublime love of Plato, the joyful visions in consciousness of Sri Aurobindo, the overflowing compassion of Paramahansa Yogananda, the wisdom of J.
Krishnamurti, the humanity of Albert Schweitzer. As
these enlightened ones walked in the footsteps of
divinity, we walked with them. All of it touched us
deeply.

An altogether new and fascinating world unfolded
when we left Austria and arrived in the United States
in 1938. With the erudite Swami Nikilhananda at the
Ramakrishna-Vivekananda Center in New York, we
studied the three component parts of ancient oriental
wisdom: Vedanta (including the Bhagavad Gita), the
different Yoga systems and Shankara's peerless *Self-
Knowledge*. Later we became familiar with Theoso-
phy and H. P. Blavatsky's *Isis Unveiled* and *The Secret Doctrine*. And, of course, we studied all of C. W.
Leadbeater's inspired books, from *The Masters and
the Path* to *Man Visible and Invisible*. With great joy
we explored Rudolf Steiner's spiritual science of
Anthroposophy, and experienced an unforgettable
performance of Goethe's *Faust* in Dornach, Switzer-
land. Later on we searched for several years through
Christian Science with Mary Baker Eddy's *Science
and Health*. Finally we came full circle to the study
of the Bible's first and last books, Genesis and Revelation.

As we shared "the Good, the True and the Beautiful" throughout those many years (a third of a cen-

tury) our thoughts often turned to the nature of love, death and the hereafter. Everything seemed so clear and simple until, in 1966, Walter passed away. It put an end to our long quest for truth and its cradle. I was left alone to face and test what the two of us had learned to believe. I began to question: could death, a change in space and time, tear asunder the bond of love between two souls when one no longer has the vehicle of mortal matter? I searched fervently for the answer and gradually it became my unshakable inner knowing: just as there is no life without death, there can be no death without life. In reality "death" is but the turning of a page in the book of life and can have no power beyond the illusion of form. Real *love*, therefore, has no spaces that separate. It is timeless, and its hereness lives on, and has lived on and on.

Soon thereafter, and true to an old saying, "when the pupil is ready, the teacher appears," a great metaphysical Teacher and eminent Kabbalist came my way and accepted me as his only personal student of "the Tree of Life." This totally unexpected happening marked a supreme turning point on all levels of my life and brought new dimensions of untold joy, inspiration and fulfillment. In good time I came to realize that all the great truths, or "faces of God" as Walter called them, which I had pursued for so long, were but footprints that led me to the reality of truth as illustrated and told by the ancient wisdom-glyph. Step by step the Tree of Life pattern unfolded the ultimate foundation of life and illustrated that primordial truth which is beyond words. Because, as my Teacher often repeated, "a truth explained in everyday words is a truth no longer true."

Like a close friend, my Teacher shared his profound knowledge and wisdom with me. He had but one stipulation—that his name would never be given to anyone. I have always honored this request, and thus I refer to him here only as "my Teacher." He gave of himself abundantly in the many informal dialogues which he preferred to conventional "classroom" instruction. For more than seven years our regular meetings took place every four or five weeks depending on my Teacher's time. They lasted for one hour and were always recorded on tape. The intervals between meetings gave me enough time to contemplate and study the last discourses thoroughly and formulate my next questions. The frame of the teachings represented the oral tradition and came largely from what is called the Unwritten Kabbalah, a body of wisdom formerly entrusted to a select few. Sometimes they followed the Mystical Kabbalah, which tells of the nature of the Creator, and his creation, the universe and humanity.

Gradually I came to understand the all-pervading "Laws of Life" which move all manifestation in universal harmony. Most importantly, I began to feel the freedom they generate in myself. Again and again my Teacher stressed the urgent need for human freedom as the very essence and purpose of Life's Great Plan. And by pointing to the Tree of Life for a practical road map, he explained how everyone can quite naturally reach that independence if only he or she so chooses.

Under the guidance of my Teacher, the unknown became knowable, the invisible visible and the unfamiliar familiar. "There is no place where life is not," he used to say. "Life, as *love*, cannot *be* without free expression. All that is visible to our senses is only a vivid display and proof of the invisible from which it came."

In time, life's vibrant and glorious beat manifested stronger. No longer was I merely an interested but passive observer of the world around me. I became an active and most enthusiastic participant in the fullness of a greater life. The Tree of Life—a tangible symbol—had become a living part of me.

My first seminars and workshops on the Tree of Life began in 1974. After seven years of study with my Teacher, Pir Vilayat Inayat Khan, the head of the Sufi Order of the West, asked me to teach the Kabbalah to his Sufi groups in the United States and in Chamonix, France. I had the good fortune of meeting the Pir in 1973. In 1974, he initiated me into the Order, founded in 1919 in Paris by his father Hazrat Inayat Khan. He gave me the name of Rabi-a al-'Adawiyya, the eighth-century mystic of Basra and first woman Sufi saint. My seminars on the Tree of Life steadily expanded into wider circles, and they still continue to grow.

Slowly I discarded my other self, the Ann Williams-Heller, a practical, successful writer and lecturer on nutrition and food. Financial gains and professional recognition, which once seemed so important, no longer drove me to remain on top.

Today, twenty years after I started to climb the Tree of Life, my workshop-seminars and the very close contact with so many young and young-at-heart "seekers of eternity" add one more purpose to my full life in this great world of adventure, wonderment and love.

If I were to tell in a few words what changes the Tree of Life has brought into my life, I would say: It is a self-reliant freedom with a joy that is resonant in me everyday. I have learned to see where I had not looked before, and to hear where I had not listened before. I am awake and aware of the alluring Laws of Life which keep this restless universe in balance. And, most importantly, I have found my very own "home in the Oneness of love." For love is the great all-sustaining power that moves the sacred music of creation into its most sacred space—the human heart. Now my mind and heart can no longer doubt or fear. I feel the reason and the purpose of my life. I know where I came from, where I want to go, and to whom I am responsible. With the ways of the Tree of Life you, too, may find meaningful answers to the riddles of your life in the reality—yes, the reality—of freedom.

That is what this book is all about. Here and now, it is your book. Keep it close. Let it become the loving teacher of your yesterdays, the helpful companion of your todays and the true friend of your tomorrows. My byline is that of a faithful scribe who, with joyful heart, shares the bounty of what so lovingly was given and so gratefully received: The Tree of Life.

A. W. H.

Note: Ann Williams-Heller died in 1989 before this book was edited. Her student Karen Goodrum has made some revisions requested by the publisher. —ED.

I
How No Thing Becomes Every Thing

Figure 1. The Tree of Life and Its Paths

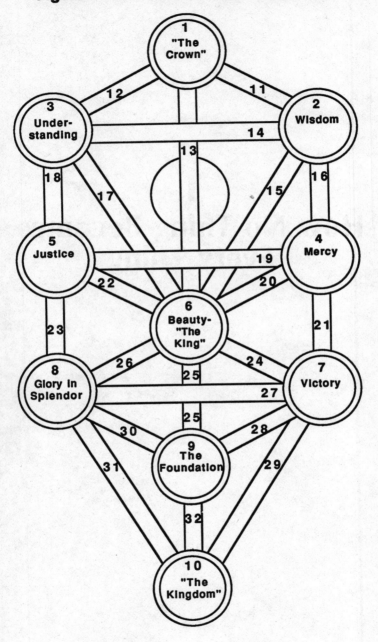

*In Understanding Our-
selves, we Embrace the
Universe; and in Contem-
plating the Universe, we
find Our Innermost Self,
so says the Tree of Life.*

1

Paving the Way

No matter where we start the story of the Tree of Life,
we are in the very midst of it. *Always*. The tale is both
complicated and simple. At first, it is like wading in
the shallow waters where the ocean meets the shore,
trying to get beyond the surf to enjoy the rhythmic
waves of the open sea. In "shallow waters" it is complicated; in "deep waters" it becomes simple, easy
and immensely rewarding.

In the beginning, unfamiliar thoughts may seem
far away. But very soon these "distant ideas" become
near and familiar through their many relationships.
Like missing parts of a jigsaw puzzle, they fall into
place and unfold a spectacular panoramic view: The
Tree of Life. (See Figure 1 and Table 1.) It tells the
enchanting Story of Life from its far-distant origin to
its far-distant future, from its invisible creator to its
appointed heir and co-creator, the visible, breathing
person. In equal measure everywhere, the same One
Spark of Life permeates everything with the same
urgency to move, the same impulse to reproduce it-

Table 1

THE TEN BRANCHES OF THE TREE OF LIFE
(A Summary)

The Number	Title		God-Name	Cosmic Sound Meaning	Sphere of
	English	Hebrew			
One	"The Crown"	Kether	Eheieh	I Am That I Am I Shall Be There	The Prime Mover
Two	Wisdom	Chokmah	Jehovah	The Lord	The Zodiac (Uranus?)
Three	Understanding	Binah	Jehovah Elohim	God of Gods The Lord God	Saturn (Neptune)
Four	Mercy/Abundance	Chesed/Gedulah	El	God, The Mighty One	Jupiter
Five	Severity/Justice	Geburah/Din/Pachad	Elohim Gebor	God of Battles God Almighty God the Potent	Mars (Pluto, Neptune?)
Six	Beauty—"The King"	Tiphareth	YHVH, Aloah va Daath	God the Strong	Sun
Seven	Victory/Firmness	Netzach	Jehovah Tzabaoth	The Lord of Hosts	Venus
Eight	Glory in Splendor	Hod	Elohim Tzabaoth	The God of Hosts	Mercury
Nine	The Foundation	Yesod	Shaddai El Chai	The Almighty Living ONE God	Levanah the Moon
Ten	"The Kingdom"	Malkuth	Adonai Malekh	The Lord and King The Lord Made Manifest in Nature	The Four Elements The Seven Planetary Powers

self. It is the nature of humanity to perceive, challenge and enjoy this significant oneness. It is likewise the nature of the Tree of Life to unfold this magnificent tale with graphic eloquence and startling surprises.

Expect therefore the unexpected. By asserting the duality of all manifestation, the Tree of Life shows how and why every event in the chain of life has two intertwined meanings. One is its individual significance, the other is its relationship to the overall whole. Thereby it uncovers humankind's intimate cosmic link with that supreme life-force without definition which words cannot express and whose personified glorious majesty many call God. The Tree of Life will therefore always tell two tales in one single breath: One is the story of humanity in the universe, the other the story of the universe in humanity.

It is always "as above so below; as below so above." Known as the Hermetic Rule, this self-evident truth is attributed to Hermes Trismegistus.[1] The saying illustrates the eternal Law of Correspondences which states that the manifest macrocosmic universe imprints its objective reflection on the microcosmic human being. And the converse is equally true: whatever manifests in the human body, mind, soul and spirit finds its vibratory correspondence in the universe at large.

And there is more. As the creation of the universe unfolds, it presents at the same time a peerless and very special diary. It is the story of You—the real You behind the sometimes misleading matter-husk that carries your name tag. By showing how the cosmic heartbeat harmonizes your life, this diary highlights the many subtle relationships with your innermost self, your fellows, your environment, and the rest of the interdependent oneness of life. In other words, you may experience that precious and unique You of which C. G. Jung said, "What is closest to you is the very thing you know least about."

Expect more of the unexpected. It is the Tree of Life which, by narrating the metaphysical government of the universe and life itself, surveys and explains the Laws of Life in motion. Far more powerful than any structured earthly law, this cosmic precision-network of interrelated power vibrations lies unrevealed behind everything experienced in the mundane mirror of form. Though the Laws of Life are not physically manifest, their patterns of order and unity move all that is manifest in self-regulating ways.

In striking parallels, the Tree of Life illustrates their co-equality, their contrary qualities, their meaning, reason and purpose, their origin and nature. With the branches of the Tree as guiding lights, we can understand and follow universal law and order behind our terrestrial disorder, and thus go beyond what our senses see, hear, smell, touch and taste. The great mystic Meister Eckhart considered our oneness with the Laws of Life of paramount importance, because their power is one with us. When we are in harmony with the universe, we can solve our daily problems constructively. Thus, The Tree of Life applies its perennial wisdom[2] practically to the bewildering happenings in our confused world while remaining ever faithful to its venerable tradition. (For a historical background of the Tree of Life and its central place in the Kabbalah, the Appendix (page 237) tells the story behind the story.

Paving the way a little further, and to separate fact from fiction, here are a few words about what the Tree of Life is and what it is not.

The Tree of Life does not present a religion but a
revealed truth which is at the core of all world religions and universal thoughts. It is not an object of
worship, as many symbols are. It is not a doctrine of
faith but a message of life. It has no dogma, no creed,
no ceremony. It occupies no place in space. It has no
magical powers. It demands no sacrifice. It is no
longer locked away as a secret treasure for a select
few. Its profound, yet practical, wisdom belongs to
all earnest searchers after genuine truth . . . here and
now.

Both visually and literally, the Tree of Life is a way
of life, a way of living, a way of thinking, a way of
relating, a way of awakening, a way of self-discovery,
a way of sharing. Its wisdom-path is ready to lead the
human mind from personal to universal awareness,
and to direct the soul from a magnetic earth-con-
sciousness to the cosmic consciousness of the heart.

The Tree of Life raises your transcendental outlook
and sharpens your insight of what, deep down, you
already *are*. Equally important, it never prescribes a
solution. Rather, it pinpoints existing conflicts of
thoughts, feelings and actions. Therefore, no matter
what your religious denomination, or what system of
thought you may follow—that of a devout Hindu,
Buddhist, Jew, Christian or Muslim, of an independent individualist, a so-called atheist or a mystic—
the Tree of Life will provide the script to plan your
spiritual future.

Most importantly, the Tree of Life provides a visual chart, a cosmic pattern, a map of what lies within
the macrocosm (the universe) and the microcosm
(human beings). It tells the story of the universe's
reason and purpose for existence, which is likewise
your own life's reason and purpose. In essence, it
illustrates the invisible network of power vibrations

(the immutable Laws of Life) which—in their manifold and often conflicting interrelationships—keep the universe in the balanced harmony of *universal freedom*. On the human level (and the one emphasized throughout this book) this balanced harmony expresses itself as *your personal freedom*—your undeniable heritage in the Great Plan of Life.

My teacher summed it up with these words: "The Tree of Life illustrates how to meet life, *your full life*. Look, therefore, at spiritual matters as though they were mundane. And respond to terrestrial problems as though they were spiritual. *This then is your wondrous journey from Sense to Soul!*"

*That which has been is
Now; and That which Is to
Be has already Been; and
God Requires That which
is Past.*
Ecclesiastes 3:15

2
The Tree of Life: Pattern of Freedom

The Tree of Life (Figure 1) is a blueprint of reality. It portrays the primary life force as it creates everything according to the immutable Laws of Life. It reveals the metaphysical pattern of both universe and humanity. On the human level, the tree-symbol becomes also the cosmic road map to trace from where you came, to show where you are now, and to point the way to your self-chosen goal. While both the glyph's remote origin and its architect remain unknown to this day, it is convincingly evident that its geometric design and story are in the purest mystic tradition, genuinely inspired, not invented.

As already mentioned, the diagram itself is simple and clear. Its interpretation is rather complex, for it pictures a vast network of cosmic relationships, which in their incessant rhythmic motion, keep the universe and humankind in floating harmony. Existence is moving into life.

Untouched by the ebb and flow of time, the Tree of

9

Life's perennial wisdom and profound knowledge is as new as the day. By harmoniously blending the mundane and the metaphysical in simple and constructive ways, it always applies itself to everyday events; always facing the tension-packed lifestyles of modern people, always exploring the most vexing questions, always meeting the intricate conflicts of our times.

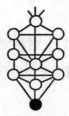

The exterior of the Tree has three distinct parts: roots, branches and paths. The three small lines on top are the roots. The ten equal-sized globes form the branches. The twenty-two lines that connect the branches are called paths. The dark dot in the diagram indicates where, metaphysically, you are now: on the last branch of the Tree of Life, which is the phenomenal world of matter and action, the Earth plane.

From the human viewpoint, the Tree of Life expresses—again!—a twofold story. One is the descent of the cosmic self from the supreme unity that embodies all things to physical life on earth; the other is the ascent to divinity. And in so doing, the diagram describes the nature of the metaphysical (inner) one who, according to the great Sufi poet Ibn 'Arabi (1165-1240), is the "created Creator" and not a created creature. As the Tree uncovers your inner space, it recaptures your ever-present past with its precious legacy and noble birthright. It shows your indispensable role and ultimate purpose in the evolution of the universe, which in turn leads the way to true independence. This very personal freedom is a state of genuine, dynamic selfhood, unrestricted by time and space, universal and clear of terrestrial limitations. It is an inner knowing, a self-fulfilling security which, when uncovered, will provide your "open sesame" to a meaningful life.

Not surprisingly, the ten branches of the Tree of Life represent a set of interwoven human qualities, attainable through natural, metaphysical self-synthesis—not by dissecting self-analysis. This unique "cosmic psychology" applies simultaneously on transcendental (metaphysical) and the terrestrial (physical) levels. It tells pictorially how humankind perceives, imparts, shares and fulfills its global partnership responsibilities for its own progress, harmony and freedom, as well as that of the universe. For this reason the Tree of Life is often named "Humanity's Pathway to Freedom."

With powerful symbols,[3] the picture language of ancient mysteries and myth, the Tree of Life tells of that ultimate truth which words could not express. "Symbols reflect reality. Like bright candles, they put light on that which otherwise would remain unseen," my Teacher often remarked.

Actually, the Tree of Life diagram is the symbol of yet another, and perhaps the most ancient of all known universal images: the Cosmic Tree of Life.[4] It relates, of course, to the tree in the Garden of Eden. Like all trees in the cosmology of other sacred scriptures, the biblical Tree of Life marks the beginning of creation, and promises the continuity of life. However, the meaning of our pictograph is so diversified and so multi-faceted that it adds its own cosmic magnitude and fascination to the silent World Tree of Life.

Because of its mandala-like symmetry, the Tree of Life diagram divides naturally into several harmonious patterns. Patterns are cosmic designs that are constant and repeat themselves with regularity, such as the sound of musical chords and harmonies, the decad of numbers and the sevenfold rainbow spectrum. The human body follows its own unique pattern of bones, tissues, organs and fluids, a pattern which stretches from birth to death. The major glands follow the energies of the centers of inner consciousness, known as chakras. The body is patterned by the four elements of life: fire, water, air, and earth. Our terrestrial days follow yet another personal pattern whose meaning the wandering stars project into the space of the zodiac. Some of the patterns in the Tree of Life include the Four Worlds, the Trinities, the Three Pillars and the Seven Planes of Existence (Figure 2). Each explores the Tree of Life's inner spaces and provides spiritual insights for daily living.

A closer look at the Tree of Life (described on pages 33-88) shows the following four distinct hallmarks, each with a twofold meaning: its own individual significance and its relationships.

1. The Tree is inverted.[4] Its hidden roots reach upward, and its branches unfold downward. The meanings are: First, all life comes from above and is continuously sustained by that which "is" above. Second, what we notice as the world around us, though real as such, is not what it appears to be.

As to the first meaning, Plato said that "the soul of

man is an inverted tree." Also, and interestingly, the giant African baobab tree appears to have its roots in the air. According to legend, God himself planted the baobab tree as a permanent habitat for countless kinds of birds and monkeys.

The second meaning of the upside-down tree must not be confused with the Hindu concept of Maya, erroneously called "illusion." All told, and in spite of prodigious advances in science and technology, we still see but a very limited slice of the total universe. And while we can look objectively at the world around us (at a flower or a landscape, for example), we can never see ourselves as we really are. In a quiet mountain lake, we see ourselves factually upside down. In a mirror we see only our reflected image. And if the flower could look into a mirror, it too would see only its mirror image: a relative reality.

2. The three roots of the Tree are hidden behind the veils of the Great Beyond, which we shall explore in the next chapter. The meanings are: First, life's true origin will always be a mystery. Second, the origin of what we experience as the "now" lies hidden in our distant past. In other words, hindsight makes the dim past immediate in the here and now. The vitally important steps ahead depend in great measure on what has been learned from the past. This is why my Teacher so frequently stressed, *"Take along the past! Yesterday is always your teacher. It is always your companion today and your friend tomorrow. Today is always the tomorrow you built yesterday."*

3. All branches of the Tree grow directly from the roots and have neither trunk nor stem. The meanings are: First, life, though manifest in matter, is directly sustained by its primal origin. Second, without a stem, it is possible to maintain the closest contact between all Tree branches.

4. The Tree branches are linked in two ways:[5] (1)

Inwardly, by the Path of the Lightning Flash, and (2) outwardly, by the twenty-two Paths of Wisdom (Figure 3). The first pattern is objective and illustrates the original qualities of life in evolution. The second pattern is subjective; it shows the two-way relationships which exist not only between all Tree branches but also in our personal life experiences.

Figure 2. The Tree of Life: Division into Harmonious Patterns

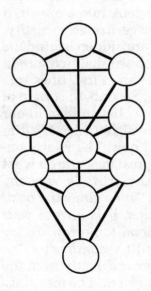

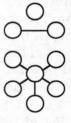
Four Worlds

The Trinities

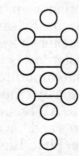
Three Pillars   Seven Planes

Figure 3. The Tree of Life
Two links between its Branches

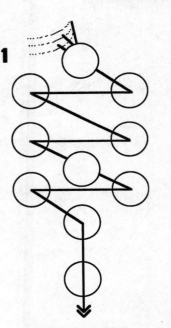

1

The Pathway of Life

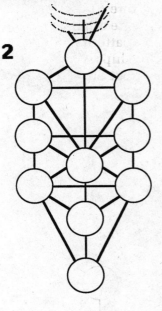

2

The Network of Cosmic
Relationships

3

Glimpses of Beginnings

To understand the Tree of Life and, in fact, our own life, we must start long before all manifest beginning. There, in the infinite shade of nonexistence and wrapped in protecting veils, three "tree roots" grow in the one and only reality that *is*: the Great Beyond. Whatever magnitude of space you can conceive, this infinity is larger.

The finite mind cannot grasp infinity. It can neither comprehend a state of non-being nor form mental pictures of it. The mind can describe infinity only with such words as beginningless, endless, formless, spaceless, timeless, causeless, measureless and soundless.

The Great Beyond is that which has not yet occurred. It is that time-and-matter-free reality which is the mysterious source and bedrock of life-to-be. It is the causeless cause behind the cause which awaits expression, because "the reason of the existence of existence is existence itself." The same idea is expressed in the image of a serpent biting its tail. For

17

the ancient Eastern mandala (circle) illustrates how eternity moves itself; namely, according to Kundalini-yoga, as a "coiled one" sleeping in the lowest of the seven chakras.

Sages coined their own words to express the ultimate reality of the Great Beyond. They call it Unmanifest Existence for its complete negation, Absolute Silence for its totality of sound, the Great Zero for its sum total of numbers, the fullness of the Great Void for its non-materiality, and the Absolute at Rest for its cosmic breath inhaled. It is the Night of Brahma to Hindus, the Tao of Lao-Tzu for ancient China, the Cause of all Causes in Aristotle's Greece, and the wind-sound H-U to Sufis.

While it cannot be seen, heard or reached, the deep silence of the Great Beyond touches the mystic's meditative heart. This supreme experience is Samadhi to Hindus, Nirvana to Buddhists, Satori to Zen mystics, Union with God for Jews and Christians, and Divine Ecstasy (hahut) to whirling dervishes. But to humankind at large, Unmanifest Existence remains incomprehensible, unthinkable and unspeakable—a deep mystery.

Not so for those who know the Tree of Life. To them, the Unmanifest is only out of sight. Just as invisible light makes visible that on which it shines, so do the names of the three root-veils give indirect evidence in coded messages. Accordingly, the Great Beyond is vibrantly alive like a pregnant woman's womb. As we begin to see the origin of things, we also see the truth in the secret of things.

Above the Tree of Life, three veils in the Great Beyond act as filters to safeguard the absolute purity of the three Tree roots. Named *No-Thing* (*Ain*, in

Hebrew), the first veil signifies absolute nothingness. The second veil, called *Every-Thing* (*Ain Soph*, in Hebrew), indicates the opposite: limitless, undifferentiated expansion of all things without description, in neverending abundance. The third veil, named *Radiant Darkness and Limitless Light* (*Ain Soph Aur*, in Hebrew), points to ambivalent, if not altogether opposing, forces that exist side by side . . . with darkness as the absence of all colors and light as their presence.

Thus we find that polarity exists in the unmanifest veils. There *everything* evolves out of *nothing* and in its turn gives birth to *some other*, and again and again to some other thing that stands in opposition. Duality (the indispensable cosmic polarity) is the golden thread woven through all the branches of the Tree of Life. As one of the distinct Laws of Life, it emphasizes the perennial twin aspects of life which make our terrestrial existence so complicated, so challenging, so mysterious, and yet so very rewarding.

The Law of Polarity reveals that division is at the beginning of all things. Everything that reaches manifestation is polarized and manifests as "either/or." It is either active (+) or passive (-), acting or reacting, emitting or receiving, masculine or feminine, electric or magnetic. Fundamentally in contrast but not in conflict, these opposing qualities do not mingle. Light and shadow manifest together, as in music, sound and pause (silence) are inseparable as counterparts. It is like two people waltzing; one steps forward as the other steps back.

Sometimes polarities act as inseparable twins. To release light and heat, electrical currents need both positive and negative poles, and for stability electrically neutral atoms need an equal measure of positively charged and negatively charged electrons. In perpetual interaction, polarity is the key to understanding the ever-switching experiences of human life. The "other" is always the starting point of an "either" awareness. Like looking at the flip side of a coin, we need to know the negative before we can fully measure the value of the positive. We must experience unhappiness to fully enjoy happiness and suffer sickness to truly cherish good health.

Returning to the nature of the Great Beyond—it is like a gigantic circle, so vast that its circumference is nowhere, and its center everywhere. It vibrates at such immeasurable speed that it focuses in a point, as hurricanes do. By its own velocity this ever-whirling point turns into a glowing spark . . . ignites itself . . . bursts into a flaming line and . . . erupts a beginning as pure brilliant light. And thus the Great Beyond exhales light which does not mingle nor change

Figure 4. The Path of the Lightning Flash

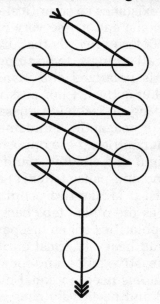

nor react. The Day of Brahma dawns . . . non-being becomes being . . . existence manifests . . . the formless becomes force . . . infinity touches eternity . . . and life starts with a radiant flash of shadowless light, the dynamic Lightning Flash of Creation (Figure 4).

Light becomes life without end. Its nature is metaphysical, not physical. Preceding the sun and stars, the universal lightning flash is not a one-time event; it emanates perpetually. Translucence dims its brilliance to protect the eyes of us mortals from turning blind. Yet our visible sunrays reflect the invisible primordial Light of Life. "Let there be light: And there was light" (Genesis 1:3).

Can physical eyes ever glimpse the invisible within the outwardly visible? Look deep into the eyes of a fellow human being, and see your own (invisible) soul reflected in your brother's or sister's eyes.

4

The Tree of Life Appears

From on high where infinity and eternity meet, the
Lightning Flash of Life bursts forth. It is an everlasting blaze. The beginning of its light knows no beginning, its end has no ending. Like nature's thunder-
bolt, it zigzags down a vertical course, then vanishes
from sight. On its way the Lightning Flash emanates
ten equal-sized globes of light. They form the
branches of the Tree of Life.

The Tree of Life is a Tree of Light. Its branches
appear and succeed one another unceasingly, like
ten candles in a row in which the flame of one kindles the next and yet remains lit. Being forever tied
to the primordial source of the one everlasting
Light—just as sunrays are tied to the sun—the self-
luminous power of the Tree branches can never fade
or fragment. Constituting the basic metaphysical ma-
terials for perpetual creation, their light shines
through all that is, but remains unseen by mortal
eyes. As the branches grow—developing step by step
in time, yet manifesting simultaneously in space—

23

they establish the pattern by which existence progresses and life evolves. According to this cosmic blueprint and architecture, the universe unfolds and fulfills its meaning and purpose.

The ten branches of the Tree of Life are named *sephiroth*, which is the plural of the Hebrew word *sephirah*. In literal translation, it means "numerical emanation." Since Hebrew root-verbs often have several meanings, *sephirah* can be variously interpreted as numbering, numerical relationship, that which is counted, light which shines, that which is related, and the voice out of nothing. Because there is no single satisfactory rendering in the English language, the Hebrew word *sephirah* is retained throughout this book and used interchangeably with its English name, its number, or simply with "Tree branch."

It is important to keep in mind that a Tree branch is an emanation, not a creation. Its continuous reappearance has an unabated quality because it is eternally linked to the Lightning Flash of Creation. By contrast, a creation is an original and thereby subject to birth, growth, decay and death.

As the Tree branches emanate along the Path of the Lightning Flash, the first and fundamental Law of Life—the Law of Change or Progression—is evident. Simply stated, this law decrees that each manifest thing moves along its own pattern and changes as it moves. Yet collectively, and in spite of their sharply contrasting qualities, the ten sephiroth are as one, a harmonious team at all times. They participate in equal measure, equal power and equal importance in the Tree's perpetual unfoldment and progress. While individually independent, they are collectively interdependent and codependent. No one Tree branch could replace any other, nor in fact be able to function without the other nine. Here the Law of Rhythm affirms that everything, including the firmament and your inner spaces, moves at its own pace, yet always in harmony with the totality of life.

Even though the density of the Tree's branches increases gradually from the second to the last, this change in no way alters the power of their inherent qualities. It is like a swimming pool which is ten feet deep at one end and tapers down to two feet at the other end—beneath the surface the water is always the same.

The manifold properties of each individual Tree branch are so complex and so diversified that no general description, no matter how detailed, could pretend to be all-inclusive; except that each sephirah represents one revealed attribute of the Creator whose total reality, however, remains forever veiled in the Great Beyond.

What every Tree branch has in common with all the others is that it is primarily a number and thereby basically nonambiguous.[6] It is a sphere of light, of sound and of movement manifesting as both rhythm and vibration. Its color is of the rainbow spectrum. Its name is a sound chosen by the Lord-God and on record in the scriptures (Old Testament). For example, the name "Eheieh" (the "I Am that I Am") of the first Tree branch is found in Exodus 3:14.

Moreover, every sephirah is all of the following: a transmitter of light, an infinite intelligence, a building block of the universe, a vibrant quality of both the Creator and creation, a center of dynamic natural force, a sphere of energy transformation, a vessel containing the primordial essence, a "space" of cosmic evolution, a "station" of wisdom, and an ever-whirling condition of existence in the universe and in us. Though this listing may sound like a chain of empty words, it is—for the time being—intended to enumerate some of the many qualities of the Tree branches. As we grow into the world of the Tree of Life, these same words will carry clear and simple meaning and indeed enhance our understanding.

As each Tree branch (except the first) emerges from the one before and instantly emits the one to follow, there is an incessant internal change, like rhythmic in-and-out breathing. Here we meet the Law of Cause and Effect in action. Each branch alternates continuously between being the effect of the one preceding it and the cause of the one that succeeds it. Expressed differently, there is a perpetual change from "being" to "becoming"—from being a cause of life to becoming an effect, and from being an effect to becoming a cause again. Action and reaction are interlinked in a chain of unbroken succession. This is known as the law of karma in the Eastern tradition. Life lives on Life. We reap what we have sown.

This cyclic relationship of constantly receiving for the purpose of constantly giving is a unique *cosmic alchemy* which takes place between all (except the last) Tree branches. In the chain of alternate polarities, each branch is first passive or "feminine" (-) in relation to the one preceding it, with the desire-will to *receive* its power-light from that one; then it becomes instantly all-active or "masculine" (+), in relation to the one that follows, with the desire-will to give its power-light to that one. Still, the predominant quality of each Tree branch remains at all times either masculine or feminine in its relationship to the other nine and in accordance with its initial function in the Great Plan of Life.

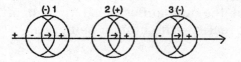

The constant polarity shifts within the first nine Tree branches go hand-in-hand with their gradual density increase. Through this step-by-step change, the infinite light in the first Tree branch "materializes" into finite life in the last. Mystics call it transformation or transfiguration. Transfiguration occurs when the all-pervading force as first cause "concretizes" into confining matter-form as its last effect. Or, to stretch this thought a little further, the palm of your hand is but the petrified expression of the imperishable spirit, which is its primal source. It is as the Sufi Master Hazrat Inayat Khan often stressed: "Spirit [an oversimplified term for "light from above"] is always fine matter, and matter is always gross spirit." The Tree of Life goes even further by illustrating that *any* terrestrial action is always a materialized thought.

A cosmic transformation can be easily witnessed in the physical changes which can occur in water. Take an open vessel with pure, briskly boiling water. Picture whitish steam rising from its surface and see it channeling through a transparent tube. The water vapor condenses slowly as a colorless liquid into another transparent container. As the liquid cools, it gradually freezes into solid ice. Whether vapor, liquid, or solid, it is always the same water, yet in a different form, expression or density. Keep this symbolic change of water in mind as the Tree of Life unfolds its cosmic transfiguraton of light into life.

Be aware also that just as the Tree branches make the invisible Creator visible and attest to the oneness of Life amidst a kaleidoscopic diversity—so does the reality of the unmanifest lead to and affirm that manifest reality—the human being, us.

Individually the ten Tree branches are unique and distinctly different. To repeat, some of their qualities are so dissimilar and contradictory that they are known as "pairs of opposites."[7] There is a fine line of demarcation between polarity and opposition. In polarity, separation is without conflict; the catchword is "either/or." In opposition, there must always be an initial friction. Yet polarities can easily turn into pairs of opposites. You will recall that opposites— which are contraries, frictions, contradictions, or resistances—are already at work in the Great Beyond where everything confronts nothing, and brilliant light opposes radiant darkness.

Basically, opposites are complements in disguise; they are allies, not enemies. Like two river banks, they are but two aspects or effects of one single cause. On the Tree of Life they are apparently conflicting unlikes with the tendency to attract, resist and complement one another. They have a significant twofold purpose: (1) to divide and separate, in order (2) to join and unite. In so doing, they actually bring about action, harmony and progress.

In all the fullness and interlocking splendor that we fail to comprehend, the ten branches of the Tree of Life—though apparently in conflict—are always a oneness in diversity, always a harmonious unity without uniformity, always in the dynamic state of total comprehension without conformity.

As previously mentioned, the perpetual polarity-interchange in the Tree of Life's branches creates harmony and promotes progress. And in accordance with the Laws of Life, the stability and evolution of each Tree branch (as of the entire universe) is maintained by constant frictions and changes within. On the mundane level this means two things: there can be no lasting progress without struggle, and only through the friction of opposing forces can balance, harmony and success evolve.

II
From Light to Life
(Pathway of Creation)

What lies behind us and before us are small matters compared to what lies within us.

Ralph Waldo Emerson

5

The Ten Tree-of-Life Branches Unfold

This section records the details of the ten branches of the Tree of Life. It illustrates (1) the constitution of the universe, (2) the metaphysical and physical anatomy of humans, and (3) the pictograph of cosmic relationships. It gathers the necessary background for the book's fourth and largest part, "More Patterns of Freedom."

Referring to the familiar jigsaw puzzle metaphor, the many single pieces for the full picture are now being assembled. Their characteristic qualities are described in successive order and compared with neighboring branches.

Each Tree branch is introduced with its number, English name, Hebrew title and a diagram indicating its location on the Tree of Life. The names and Hebrew titles are taken from the *Zohar* since they are

not mentioned by name in *The Book of Formation*.*
They are followed by the Yetziratic text taken from
the *Thirty-Two Paths of Wisdom*, a later supplement
to *The Book of Formation* as translated by A. E.
Waite. Since the ten Tree branches count also as the
first ten Paths of Wisdom, these concise words of
"intelligence" offer additional insight for contemplation and meditation.

Each Tree branch portrayal concludes with an
overview. For easy reference it incorporates perti-
nent data from later parts of the book, such as its
orientation in the Trinities, the Celestial Hierarchies,
as well as in the Four Worlds with their symbolic
color schemes.

If you feel inclined to color your own Tree pictogram, (Figure 1) use the colors of the World of Creation, as given in each Tree description. They are the
reflected colors of nature, and traditionally recommended for meditation and study.

Those who wish to memorize the highlights of the
ten branches of the Tree of Life will find Table 1 a
helpful tool.

THE NUMBER ONE: "The Crown"
Kether in Hebrew

The Text:
"The first path is called the Admirable Intelligence, the Supreme Crown. It is the light which im-

---

The Book of Formation (*Sepher Yetzirah*) by Akiba ben
Joseph, translated from the Hebrew with annotations by
Knut Stenring, and including the *Thirty-Two Paths of
Wisdom*, published by KTAV Publishing House, Inc., New
York, New York, in 1970.

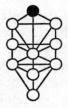

parts understanding of the beginning which is without beginning, and this also is the First Splendour. No created being can attain to its essence."

Let there be Light . . . shedding itself continuously without becoming less.

And there is brilliant, everlasting light, as the first branch of the Tree of Life emanates along the path of the cosmic lightning flash. It is the Number One. Its name is *The Crown*, the traditional emblem of royal authority, victory and triumph. It symbolizes the crowning glory of the Great Beyond from which it emerges, and heralds the radiant crown for the future King as he reigns in his Kingdom in the last Tree branch.

As the Number One, it illustrates the unknowable cause without cause out of which everything is created. It represents indivisible, partless oneness in infinite self-existence.

Its never-changing yet ever-becoming singleness *is*. It signifies the absolute undifferentiated unity in consciousness, and also the differentiated consciousness of that unity. It is "the One that is All and the One that is in All." Before the Number One, "Nothing" *is*. There are no two firsts. One multiplied by one is one, and one divided by one is one; while any number above one, divided by itself, will always return to the Number One.

The first Tree branch embodies the initiating propelling life-force, the generating energy which, in itself, is everlasting Life. Often named the Infinite, it is the motivating idea or object of thought impressing the universal mind and will. As a perpetual cosmic seed, ever-whirling toward manifestation, it is frequently illustrated as the central point of a circle which—like the acorn in an oak tree—already contains the full tree-to-be.

Kether, the creator in all great religions, symbolizes the never-changing beginning and a selfness without otherness. Pure and luminous light is creative essence pulsating in boundless, undivided space. While this undivided spaceness is without form, it will always be inherent in all manifest form. The power of its actionless existence may be considered static rather than dynamic; yet it permeates and maintains all things dynamically.

The Crown's supreme mind, infinite intelligence and sublime desire-will is beyond form, space and time. It can be voiced only in the highest measure of capitalized words as Absolute Existence, Supreme Perfection, Ultimate Unity, and Absolute Consciousness. Among its many titles are: the First Affirmation, the Beginning of All Beginnings, the Cause of All Causes, the All-containing Uncontained, the Existence of all Existences, the Holy of Holies, the Ancient of Ancients, the Footstool of God, and the Lord of Lords. As the traditional *Arik Anpin*, the Vast Countenance or Macroprosopos, it is sometimes depicted as the right-sided profile of a bearded king whose partially concealed face is still looking into the Great Beyond. Other symbols of Kether include the ever-turning wheel of life, the arcane Swastika or Fohat.

To describe the nature of the supreme One would

restrict what surpasses worldly frames and intellectual comprehension. But human beings have always passionately engaged in relating it to such ultimate qualities as Light, Life, Love, Truth and Freedom. Socrates personified it as the Good, the True and the Beautiful. For Albert Schweitzer it was the Sanctity of Life. Meister Eckhart called it the Godhead. For Sufis it is the Primal Cause and the Last Effect, and also the Light Shining from Above. It is what we call "God," and it provides the most intimate relationship a human being can have. For each person, "it" is different and unique at any time and everywhere, and always distinctly new.

To you, this "divine presence" may reveal itself as infinite mind or limitless love. To me, it may be the "One in the many," and a personal experience of the very highest impersonal power and measure. It may be found in a child's smile, a bird's song, a sunrise at the ocean's shore, or in the tears of a friend. For Moses, it was revealed in the burning bush, and to St. Paul it happened on the road to Damascus. Whatever its hallmark may be, the human heart feels that God *is* being, and not *a* being.

The first branch of the Tree of Life is the sphere of the *primum mobile* and of the first whirling center of Claudius Ptolemy. It is the Divine Pymander of Hermes Trismegistus in Egypt, and the Great Monad of Pythagoras in ancient Greece. For Northern Buddhists it is Brahma, the creator, and Atman, the one everlasting reality. It is prana and Parabrahma for the Hindus and Atmabodha for Sankaracharya. Vedantists call it "The One without a Second, eternal, immutable, stainless and pure, your innermost Self." In

Greek mythology it is the Father of all the gods; for the Persians it is Mithras, and Bel for the Chaldeans.

By analogy the sephirah Number One expresses itself in Eastern thought by the Vedantic syllable *Om*. There it is known as the sound of the universe, and pronounced A-u-m as the eternal alphabetic trinity. In Western prayers it is the Amen; in Sufi chants it is the almost silent H-U. In the Hebrew tongue it is Ruach, the cosmic mind. It is Aleph, the first letter of the Hebrew alphabet, not sounded but whispered in unvoiced breath. It is the creator's breath which permeates everything that lives. It is the very breath that God breathed into the nostrils of Adam, the first man. By divine inheritance this sacred breath is also the silent breath of life in You. Even better said: You ARE that inheritance.

Kether embraces the tender roots of the four elements of life (fire, water, air and earth), the universal building blocks of matter. Its chemical symbol is hydrogen, the first element. Its color vibration is white brilliance, which the poet Shelley named the radiance of eternity.

The divine name and cosmic sound of the first Tree branch is Eheieh, the "I Am That I Am" in Exodus 3:14, and variously translated as "I Am Who Is," "I Will Be," "I Shall Be There," and also as "The Always."

AN OVERVIEW

First Branch: The Number One

Title:
  The Crown
  Kether in Hebrew

Cosmic Sound:
  God-Name: Eheieh
  Meaning: I Am That I Am, I Shall be There, The
  Always

Figure Symbol:
  The Crown, Swastika, The Point within a Circle

Planetary Sphere: Primum Mobile (the Prime Mover)

Chemical Element/Metal: Hydrogen
  and Root of Fire, Water, Air
  and Earth

Position in:
  the Three Trinities: Supernal - Capstone
  the Three Pillars: Head of Mildness
  the Four Worlds: Origination or Emanation
                   Atziluth in Hebrew

Celestial Hierarchies:
  Archangel: Metatron, Angel of the Presence
  Order of Angels: Chaioth ha Qadesh
                   (Holy Living Creatures)
  Pseudo Dionysian (Christian): Seraphim

Symbolic Colors in the World of:
  Origination: Brilliance
  Creation: Pure white brilliance
  Formation: Pure white brilliance
  Manifestation: White flecked with gold

THE NUMBER TWO: Wisdom

Chokmah in Hebrew

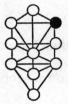

The Text:
  "The second path is called the Illuminating Intelligence. It is the Crown of Creation and the splendour of the Supreme Unity, to which it is most near in proximity. It is exalted above every head, and is distinguished by Kabbalists as the Second Splendour."

  Division is the initial impulse to creative action, and the beginning of all things.
  This second Tree branch is the Number Two. Its name is *Wisdom*. Since the Crown's indivisible godhead cannot split, it reflects solitary wisdom-light. With the appearance of this mirror image, a separation occurs in the Number Two. Polarity comes into being. Duality marks the beginning of creation.

In the first Tree branch, the supreme One is an undivided unity—all differences are excluded. The separation in the second Tree branch affirms that, to start the chain of creation in divine wisdom, differences must, and therefore do, exist. These "differences" will manifest continuously as polarity, duality and often opposition. Biblical legends dramatize their existence in proverbial family divisions, such as between Cain and Abel, Abraham and Lot, Isaac and Ishmael, Jacob and Esau. Many such allegorical separations can be found in metaphysical myths and sacred scriptures.

The Tree branch Wisdom illustrates the first actively directing cause of potential creation. Like a primal spark, it is a Vision of God, face to face, and the generating powerhouse of life.

The nature of Chokmah is threefold and rather diversified. First, by reflecting the divine qualities of Number One, Number Two reveals Pure Wisdom. By viewing the crown of Godhead in the immensity of space, its infinite wisdom is comprehended. On the mundane level, this supreme wisdom dwells in our inner space, even when unnoticed in everyday life.

Second, the undivided space of Number One (symbolized by a circle) divides into twelve uniform spokes to form the infinite wheel of the celestial Zodiac. This endless space answers the Creator's need to be revealed; and the zodiac is therefore justly considered the abode of the sacred name of the Hebrew God, the four-lettered Tetragrammaton, spelled YHVH, and sometimes written IHVH and JHWH. Curiously enough, the Tree branch Wisdom is also the home of its first letter, Yod. While in image and fact the Tetragrammaton is the eternal lock and a key to true wisdom, the single letter Yod is in turn symbolic of humans as God's appointed steward and co-creator on earth. Here also is the hall of all avatars of all ages before their human incarnation.

The third quality of this sephirah brings forth the idea of the fertilizing, mobilizing, dynamic and expanding life force, the phallic aspect and male archetype principle of gender, which is not yet sex, and which has the lingam as its symbol. It is the cosmic sperm emitted from the universal seed (contained in Number One) which illustrates the mythical maleness of husband, father, son, and brother. The manifold relationships of the male archetype constitute a primary powerhouse of life which stimulate all humankind, male and female alike, in the here and now.

By analogy, this Tree branch finds many attributes. As the "Seat of the Father," it is personified in Eastern religions by Brahma, Lord Krishna and Lord Buddha. In Greek mythology the names are Zeus, Apollo and Jupiter; and—not surprisingly—also Pallas Athena, the blindfolded goddess, emerging in full armor from the head of her father, Zeus, to exercise wisdom and justice. In Egyptian mythology it is Khepera, the self-begotten invincible god of eternities with a scarab head on a human body (which refers to the Crown of the Tree's first branch). In the Tao of Lao-Tzu it is the Yang: masculine, positive, dry and hot. It also represents the Logos, the living word of life, reflected in the Bible as "In the beginning was the word, and the word was with God" (John 1:1).

The Number Two is sometimes considered to be the abode of the explosive planet Uranus. The chemical symbol of Chokmah is uranium and all other radioactive elements. Its color vibration is iridescent gray, symbolic of the veil which dims the brilliant white of the first Tree branch.

The divine name and cosmic sound is Jehovah, The Lord.

AN OVERVIEW

Second Branch: The Number Two

Title:
  Wisdom
  Chokmah in Hebrew

Cosmic Sound:
  God-Name: Jehovah
  Meaning: The Lord

Figure Symbol:
  The Lingam (Phallus), the Tetragrammaton and its First Letter, Yod.

Planetary Sphere: The Zodiac, Uranus?

Chemical Element/Metal: Uranium

Position in:
  the Three Trinities: Supernal
  the Three Pillars: Head of Mercy
  the Four Worlds: Creation
                    Briah in Hebrew

Celestial Hierarchies:
  Archangel: Ratziel, Herald of Deity
  Order of Angels: Auphanim (Wheels)
  Pseudo Dionysian (Christian): Cherubim

Symbolic Colors in the World of:
  Origination: Pure soft blue
  Creation: Gray
  Formation: Pearl gray, iridescent
  Manifestation: White flecked with red, blue and
  yellow

THE NUMBER THREE: Understanding

Binah in Hebrew

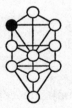

The Text:
  "The third path is called the Sanctifying Intelligence, and it is the foundation of Primordial Wisdom, termed the Creation of Faith. It is the mother of
Faith, which indeed emanates therefrom."

  Let form limit force and make space for the new:
the universal trinity.
  The third branch of the Tree of Life aims at the

three-dimensional universe, and embodies the dynamic qualities which by attraction and resistance, connect and challenge, move and transmit, harmonize and mobilize creative forces into being.

It is the Number Three, and its name is *Understanding*. It is parallel to and a co-equal of the second Tree branch. Its nature is in opposition to the latter's vibrations. For while Number Two portrays an all-begetting cosmic maleness, Number Three signifies universal womb-manness and its generating power. It personifies the passive, yet always receptive and directing "God the Mother," the preserving and reproducing giver of life and form. For within the space of Number Two, Number Three is the universal cup (with the sacred Grail chalice as its symbol), ready to receive and hold the cosmic sperm and transform its force into new life. It is thereby the female archetype principle as gender, though not as yet sex: the mythical womb-man of wife, mother, daughter and sister. This primary Womb of Life lives—like the second branch of the Tree of Life—in the here and now, and stimulates all humankind, male and female alike.

Another quality of the Tree of Life's third branch tells of the three aspects of passing time. It illustrates: (1) the virgin, (2) the fertile maiden, and (3) the already sterile, aging matron. Allegorically, womanhood is personified in its various phases, such as by Anima Mundi, pregnant with life to come, and by the great sea Mara, in which all life takes form. In Christianity, the Virgin Mary illustrates the immaculate maiden whose womb is still veiled. In Egypt her name is Isis, the worldly Queen of Heaven. And as Grecian Gaia, she represents both the mother of Uranus and the motherly matron, whose vision of sorrow deepens her intuition, her understanding and her helpfulness.

Because of the close link with the Godhead, Sufis look at womanhood as "the stepping stone to God's sacred altar." There, clothed with the sun, the moon at her feet, and a crown of twelve stars upon her head, she fulfills her divine purpose.

In the Tree branch of Understanding resides the second letter, He, of the Holy Tetragrammaton YHVH. The letter He (meaning window in Hebrew) refers to an inner knowing and also to an open outlook on life. This third sephirah is likewise the abode of the most distant classic planet Saturn. Known as the slowest marker of time, Saturn is appropriately named after the youngest son of Uranus and Gaia.

In the Tao, Understanding is the Yin: feminine, passive, damp and cold. Its chemical symbol is oxygen, the element that kindles and sustains vibrant life.

The color vibration of the Tree branch, Binah, is black, symbolic of the residing planet Saturn. The divine name and cosmic sound is Jehovah Elohim, the God of Gods.

There is a uniquely significant relationship between the second and third branches of the Tree of Life, between Chokmah and Binah, which is often called "the extreme polarity." They illustrate the mutual dependence between force and form. Each branch is in need of the other so as to fulfill itself and the other. Force (the fertilizing power of maleness) would go to waste without a form with which to hold it, while form (the cosmic cup) would remain empty without an expanding force to fill it. In short, force and form oppose *and* complement one another. Their dynamic interaction evolves as wisdom's masculine force opposes Understanding's feminine form. As the dynamic cosmic spark plug penetrates its opposite, their interdependent qualities complement one another, and the marriage of opposites takes place. Extreme polarities are links in the chain of life, and, more importantly, the movement into actual creation.

The following visual comparison of the opposites in the Two Archetypes of Creation will prove a useful tool for study and meditation.

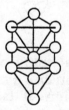

BRANCH NUMBER TWO	*BRANCH NUMBER THREE*
Wisdom (Force)	Understanding (Form)
the essence; free-moving	the substance; concreting
transmitting and fertilizing	form-giving, reproducing life-building (creating)
fast and stimulating	slow and preserving

creative and generative	receptive and generating
stirring things into action	bringing things into being
masculine gender	feminine gender

The Tree branch of Understanding is eternally linked to the Crown. And thus the first geometrical design manifests. This trinity is called the plane figure or triad.

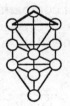

The transcendental unity of the Numbers One, Two and Three establishes a triune structure which underlies all creation. It is the oneness of the Knower, acting in balance with the Known, giving freedom to the faculty of Knowing. It is the oneness of the origin with its reflection and its established identity. In universal mind, it is an idea, a projection of the idea, and the preservation of the idea. The third part of the trinity is always that which connects and fuses and brings forth new life.

In Eastern philosophy the triune principle is expressed by the oneness of "the seer," which is the divine awareness of seeing; "the seen," which is the active principle of seeing; and "that which is seen," or the receptive faculty of seeing.

As another living symbol, the shape of the trinity

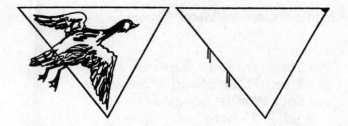

can be likened to a bird which flies freely into the boundless freedom of the sky, its head leading its wings.

It is well to remember that every human relationship has both Wisdom-Understanding *and* the triune principle at its core. Herein lies the key to all human problems. The chapter "Trinity: The Architect of Creation" will present further details on this important subject.

AN OVERVIEW

Third Branch: The Number Three

Title:
  Understanding
  Binah in Hebrew

Cosmic Sound:
  God-Name: Jehovah Elohim
  Meaning: The Lord God, God of Gods

Figure Symbol:
  The Cup, Chalices

Planetary Sphere: Saturn

Chemical Element/Metal: Oxygen

Position in:
  the Three Trinities: Supernal
  the Three Pillars: Head of Severity
  the Four Worlds: Creation
    Briah in Hebrew

Celestial Hierarchies:
  Archangel: Tzaphkiel, The Beholder of God
  Order of Angels: Aralim (Mighty Ones)
  Pseudo Dionysian (Christian): Thrones

Symbolic Colors in the World of:
  Origination: Crimson
  Creation: Black
  Formation: Dark Brown
  Manifestation: Gray flecked with pink

KNOWLEDGE—DAATH

Before the fourth branch of the Tree of Life can emanate, the Lightning Flash passes through a veil in front of an abyss. This points to a change from force to form-expression, and from a potentiality to an actuality.

Hidden behind this veil is a Tree branch without number, sound and color. It is named "Knowledge" (*Daath* in Hebrew), which, in its biblical sense, means "as a man knows his wife." This indicates the mystical union of maleness and womb-man-ness which happens on a level other than wisdom and understanding. Thereby it points to a relationship which goes beyond the biological gratification of human sex.

As viewed from earth (the tenth Tree branch), and unlike all other Tree branches, Daath is not an objective quality of divinity but rather a subjective experience concealed between its cause and its effect.

We shall come back to Knowledge-Daath in Chapter 12. For now it suffices to remember that in it hides the unrevealed secret of the Tree of Life, and also the locked-up innermost secret of your own life.

THE NUMBER FOUR: Mercy/Abundance
Chesed and Gedulah in Hebrew

The Text:
"The fourth path is called the Arresting or Receiving Intelligence, because it arises like a boundary to receive the emanations of the higher intelligence which are sent down to it. Herefrom all spiritual virtues emanate by the way of subtlety, which itself emanates from the Supreme Crown."

Creation is always on the move. It carries within itself the cosmic memory of the established trinity, the next step toward manifestation. The fourth branch of the Tree of Life is thus the gateway to visible form. It is the Number Four, named Mercy and sometimes Abundance, Majesty and Greatness. The formation of matter begins with God's signature, by virtue of the divine power of true charity. There are no mistakes or accidents in God's entire creation.

This Tree branch illustrates that motivating force is a governing principle of loving-kindness which, like a metaphysical horn of plenty, gives indiscriminately with compassion and inspiration to one and all. It represents productive and life-giving power, an expansion of will in a complete combination of ideas and thoughts. The legendary being in the figure below represents a man standing firmly erect on his inherited earthly soil with the divine trinity on his head.

Considered a lower level of Number Two, the Tree branch Mercy is beholden to the Creator's compassion and sublime will. In the terrestrial spheres, these qualities express themselves as a will to live and to love.

Analogies to this Tree branch are found abundantly wherever we look. Sometimes they mark nature's voluntary partitions. In nature there are four distinct kingdoms: the mineral, the plant, the animal and the human. A day can be divided into four equal parts, as morning, noon, evening, and night. The moon travels through four stages: increase, full, decrease and renewal. And the year, in its turn, counts four seasons: spring, summer, autumn and winter.

Love, faith and a sacred happiness are the dynamic qualities of the sephirah Mercy: love in the sense of compassion as spiritual understanding; selfless charisma; faith with its twin companions, blind belief and understanding; and happiness in the sense of serenity and spiritual fulfillment. These transcendental properties are personified by the Lord of Heaven with all the goodness and power of the righteous and benevolent ruler, the giver of gifts, the generous and loving father, the compassionate healer, and the peaceful good shepherd who watches over his flock. In Hindu mythology it personifies Vishnu, the preserver. For the Greeks, the comparable figure is Zeus, ruler over gods and humans. In human beings, the qualities of this Tree branch express themselves in a charitable care of others and in a sincere joy of sharing.

With its perfect square framework, the geometric symbols of Chesed are the solid cube, the pyramid and the tetrahedron.

The Number Four is the sphere of Jupiter, the planet of expansion and abundance. Its chemical symbol is carbon, the sturdy and plentiful energy-yielding element. The color-vibration is blue. The symbolic banner is that of Christian "faith, hope and charity."

The divine name and cosmic sound is El, The Mighty One.

AN OVERVIEW

Fourth Branch: The Number Four

Title:
 Mercy/Abundance/Majesty
 Chesed, Gedulah in Hebrew

Cosmic Sound:
 God-Name: El
 Meaning: God, the Mighty One

Figure Symbol:
 Square, Sceptre and the First Solids: Cube, Pyramid, Tetrahedron

Planetary Sphere: Jupiter

Chemical Element/Metal: Carbon

Position in:
 the Three Trinities: Ethical or Moral
 the Three Pillars: Center of Mercy
 the Four Worlds: Formation
  Yetzirah in Hebrew

Celestial Hierarchies:
 Archangel: Tzadkiel, The Righteous of God
 Order of Angels: Chasmalim (Brilliant Ones)
 Pseudo Dionysian (Christian): Dominions

Symbolic Colors in the World of:
 Origination: Deep violet
 Creation: Blue
 Formation: Deep Purple
 Manifestation: Deep azure flecked with yellow

THE NUMBER FIVE: Severity/Justice
Geburah, Din and Pachad in Hebrew

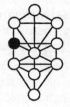

The Text:
"The fifth path is called the Radical Intelligence, because it is more akin than any other to the Supreme Unity and emanates from the depths of the Primordial Wisdom."

Justice defends and corrects. Struggle and strife purify.

Exercised to the extreme, virtue turns into vice. To prevent and correct it, the fifth branch on the Tree of Life, the Number Five, is Severity. It is often named Justice, Fortitude, and sometimes Fear in the sense of awe. Since it grows parallel to and on the same level as Number Four, it is in opposition to the vibrations of the latter. It is also the lower arc of Number Three.

"Fear in the sense of awe" means respectful acceptance of the governing principle of justice. For example, we benefit from using electricity extensively and constructively, and with a sense of awe. But if we disrespect electricity, then it can do much harm and even create destruction.

Geburah illustrates the *correcting force*, the purifying power of justice in action, the disposer of waste, the divine rigor and the cosmic broom of strength to do away with inequality and eliminate the superflu-

ous. In the realm of endurance and divine will it
represents the realistic disciplinarian, the sacrificial
priest, the dragon-slayer, the guardian of law and the
discriminating celestial surgeon who eradicates use-
less overabundance with courage, responsibility and
even sacrifice. In an indirect way, this Tree branch
introduces the awareness of good and evil, which is
humankind's destiny as well as its protection. The
pentagram or five-pointed star is therefore not only
the emblem of safety, but also the fitting figure symbol of a human standing erect with legs apart and
arms outstretched. Curiously enough, and like a human, the pentagram pattern grows in two opposite
directions: from the inside out and from the outside
in (Figure 5). No other geometric design can claim
that quality.

Whereas Number Four is the constructive will to
live, Number Five personifies the destructive will
not to live and thus the death wish postulated by
Sigmund Freud. It furthermore represents karma, the
impartial cosmic law of causality as the result of
action, not as blind fate. It illustrates the God of
vengeance whose voice resounds in the Bible as
"Vengeance is mine, I shall repay." That voice was
also the battle cry of many an ancient prophet.

This Tree branch is the residence of the planet
Mars, so named after the powerful Lord of War
whose readiness to fight adds impatience and vio-
lence to battles. In that sense, Number Five frequently indicates struggle. And yet, it is by this very friction that a person develops the strength to choose
between right and wrong and thereby attains independence. According to some experts, the more recently discovered planet Pluto is said to find a home
here. Figuratively speaking, Pluto may—as King of

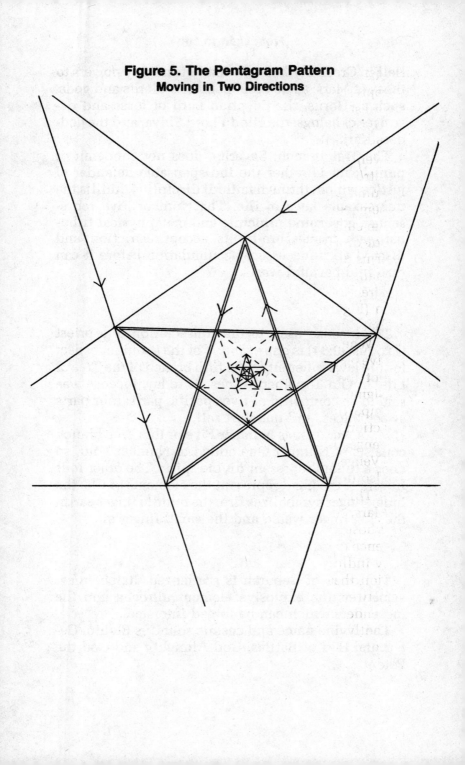

Figure 5. The Pentagram Pattern
Moving in Two Directions

Hell in Greek mythology—lend his mighty powers to those of Mars, as do other combative lords and gods, such as Horus, the Egyptian Lord of force and destroyer of beings; the Hindu Lord Shiva; and the goddess Kali.

The Tree branch, Severity, does not condemn or punish but is rather the indispensable defender of justice which, through faithful discipline, fulfills the unbreakable laws of life. The Number Five represents a governing principle and metaphysical tribunal ready to measure limits, accept restriction, and discard all unnecessary accumulation before it can turn into harmful waste.

The incense used in the consecration of a priest (Exodus 30:34) is one example of the genuine respect for the laws inherent in the fifth branch of the Tree of Life. In Old Testament times, as today, incense was said to be composed of five specific parts: four parts sweet spices, and one part salt.

Moreover, just as Number Five of this Tree branch consists of Number One added to Number Four, so does a thumb represent divine spirit. The other four fingers of the hand represent the elements of life: the index finger symbolizes fire, the middle finger earth, the ring finger water, and the small finger air.

The color of Geburah is scarlet-red. Its chemical symbol is the explosive element nitrogen and the metal iron which can be forged into steel.

The divine name and cosmic sound is Elohim Gebor, the God of Battles, God Almighty and God the Potent.

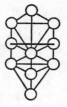

Here is a visual comparison of the opposing qualities of the Two Governing Principles of Creation.

Branch Number Four	*Branch Number Five*
Mercy	Severity
the idealist in blind obedience	the realist and his defense mechanism
affirms the good	negates the evil
love and compassion are free-flowing	immutable laws are patterned in awe
faith and truth for everybody without discrimination	justice and ethics by discrimination
the horn of plenty	the cosmic surgeon
the will to live	the will not to live
the benevolent king on his throne shares his wealth and love generously with all his people	Lord Krishna on the battlefield in his chariot directs his disciple's fierce fight against his own kin

security that *is*	self-preservation that *acts*
always balancing	always disturbing, confusing
the number of form	the number of man

AN OVERVIEW

Fifth Branch: The Number Five

Title:
  Severity/Justice
  Geburah, Din and Pachad in Hebrew

Cosmic Sound:
  God-Name: Elohim Gebor
  Meaning: God of Battles, God Almighty,
            God the Potent

Figure Symbol:
  Pentagram, Five-petaled Tudor Rose

Planetary Sphere: Mars

Chemical Element/Metal: Nitrogen, Steel, Iron

Position in:
  the Three Trinities: Ethical or Moral
  the Three Pillars: Center of Severity
  the Four Worlds: Formation
            Yetzirah in Hebrew

Celestial Hierarchies:
  Archangel: Khamael, The Severity of God
  Order of Angels: Seraphim (Fiery Serpents)
  Pseudo Dionysian (Christian): Holy Virtues

Symbolic Colors in the World of:
  Origination: Orange
  Creation: Scarlet-red
  Formation: Bright scarlet
  Manifestation: Red flecked with black

THE NUMBER SIX: Beauty "The King"
Tiphareth in Hebrew

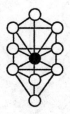

The Text:
  "The sixth path is called the Intelligence of Mediating Influence, because the flux of the emanations is multiplied therein. It communicates this affluence to those blessed men who are united with it."

Justice cannot endure without love.
  After Number Five has rightfully removed all that is unnecessary and wasteful, the sixth branch grows in the center of the Tree of Life. It is the Number Six. Named Beauty and often The King, it illustrates "the

world of the heart" where light becomes radiating love and love becomes life. Uniquely and for very good reasons, it is in direct contact with every other Tree branch except the last: our Planet Earth (Figure 6). Here the divine will (of the first branch) is especially directed toward harmony and natural balance. It is that floating serenity which Beethoven so beautifully intoned in his Sixth Symphony, the Pastorale. This Tree branch functions as mediator between the creative and governing realms above, and the functioning world of action below.

Figure 6. Links to the Heart of the Tree of Life

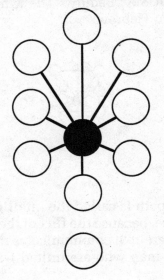

It is the home of the Holy Tetragrammaton's third letter, Vav. In Hebrew, Vav means nail. Thus, this Tree branch is the nail, which, like the word "and" in a sentence, ties and fuses the above to the below. In image and in fact, it is also the nail of voluntary sacrifice[8] which, like the legendary pelican, gave away her blood that her children might live.

From a practical point of view Tiphareth is that state of spiritual awareness, called Cosmic or Illuminated Consciousness, which one is able to attain in the present life.

By being the heart of the Tree of Life this branch marks several other turning points. In Christian tradition, the light from above starts to become life, and the Logos (the illuminated word of the Living God) starts to become flesh. It is the *Thou* facing the *I Am* from above.

On the way down the Tree and with the inflowing power of knowing, this omnipotent event is the highest sacrifice of crucifixion. Seen from below, the same event becomes the resurrection through crucifixion when—with the outflowing power of love— the son of Man becomes the Son of God. Said differently, this branch of the Tree of Life expresses two separate yet intertwined events: First the godhead's *infinite* desire and will to accept limitation and manifest in finite human flesh; and then the voluntary and utmost sacrifice of the physical body. This free, unlimited and unconditional surrender leads to resurrection on the direct path to the Godhead.

The sixth branch is the abode of all avatars and great teachers of the world, known and unknown, in

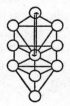

their human incarnation. With Rama, Krishna, Osiris, and Gautama the Buddha among them, they all experienced the agony of complete surrender and sovereign sacrifice. Other religions include the names of their sun gods as Ra in Egypt, Surya in India, and Ormuzd in Persia.

Beauty, the King, has many symbolic meanings. In its relation to Mercy and Severity it is the majestic King (sometimes called Thou), wearing the Crown from Number One. Likewise, it is Jesus as King of the Jews on his way down from Mount Olive on Palm Sunday. It is Gautama Buddha reaching enlightenment and Lord Krishna becoming the all-knowing. In relation to Wisdom (father) and Understanding (mother), Number Six becomes the Child, the newborn babe in Bethlehem; and Krishna as Impala, the playful child.

Its geometrical figure is the hexagram, the interlaced double triad, sometimes called the Philosopher's Diamond and also known as the Star of David. Its title is Zoar Anpin, the Lesser Countenance which is in contradistinction to Arik Anpin, the Vast Countenance of Kether.

The representative color of Number Six is golden yellow. Its planetary sphere is the Sun, the giver of life, light and warmth. Its symbolic mineral is gold, the mystical tarnish-free "precious stuff" that the alchemists of old so eagerly tried to concoct.

The divine name and cosmic sound is Aloha Va Daath which translates as, "God the Strong, God Made Manifest in the Flesh, God Manifest in the Mind and Heart of Man."

Before Number Six emanates the next Tree branch, the cosmic Lightning Flash crosses another veiled abyss. It is considered the parallel or close match to the veil hiding Knowledge-Daath. Called the Veil of Paroketh and sometimes also the Rainbow Bridge, it separates the six creating and governing branches in the divine world above from the four creatively functioning branches in the terrestrial world below (Figure 7). It is the veil between the body and the soul which was rent in twain at the moment of Christ's crucifixion (Matthew 27:51 and Mark 15:38). Therefore, it is frequently referred to as the "Veil of the Temple."

Figure 7. The Veil of Paroketh

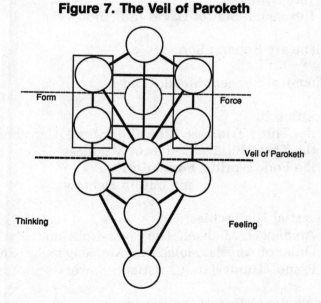

AN OVERVIEW

Sixth Branch: The Number Six

Title:
 Beauty-The King
 Tiphareth in Hebrew

Cosmic Sound:
 God-Name: Aloah Va Daath
 Meaning: God the Strong

Figure Symbol:
 Hexagram, Star of David (Solomon's Seal)

Planetary Sphere: Sun

Chemical Element/Metal: Gold

Position in:
 the Three Trinities: Ethical or Moral, Capstone
 the Three Pillars: Center of Mildness
 the Four Worlds: Formation
                          Yetzirah in Hebrew

Celestial Hierarchies:
 Archangel: Michael, The Perfect of God
 Order of Angels: Malachim (Messengers or Kings)
 Pseudo Dionysian (Christian): Powers

Symbolic Colors in the World of:
 Origination: Clear rose-pink
 Creation: Golden yellow
 Formation: Rich salmon-pink
 Manifestation: Golden amber

THE NUMBER SEVEN: Victory/Firmness
Netzach in Hebrew

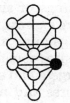

The Text: *"The seventh path is called the Hidden Intelligence because it pours out a brilliant splendour on all intellectual virtues which are beheld with the eyes of the spirit and by the ecstasy of faith."*

"How do I love thee? Let me count the ways," wrote Elizabeth Barrett Browning

The seventh branch of the Tree of Life, named Victory and sometimes Firmness, is the Number Seven. As we shall find throughout the pages of this book, the digit Seven occupies a special place in the numerical system and does so for many good reasons.

Netzach releases floods of powerful, formless and uninhibited emotions, which manifest four ways—as instinct, intuition, desire, and a tempting, romantic, and at times even sensuous quality of love.

Instinct, a natural, instantaneous and reactive impulse, is unconscious knowledge. It knows but knows not why. It acts below the level of discrimination and responds more or less automatically within individual patterns.

Intuition, a direct and foolproof perception of something true, brings immediate pure, productive and unerring insight. It is an inner knowing without reasoning. Intuition is frequently confused with imagination, which in its turn is a creation of the mind. My Teacher pinpointed the difference by saying, "Imagination is human, intuition is divine."

Desires are yearnings of any kind, and of every measure. Every desire expresses a need existing in its background. When genuine and strong, desires are self-revolving. If desires remain unheeded, they become all the more urgent and apparent. Then vicious cycles between desires and needs are formed, and their strength increases steadily.

Desires are of the earth. Their power can break down barriers. Therefore, the stronger your desire, the greater is your strength to reach your aim and goal. It has been said that a one-pointed desire is the strongest prayer of all.

Sufis have their own way to look at their four basic desires: the desire to know, the desire to love and be loved, the desire for joy, and the desire for peace. Should any one of these four remain unfulfilled, a heavy heart will tell the tale. Every desire is an emotional hunger for freedom. It may be freedom from bodily hunger, freedom from loneliness, or anything in between.

Love is without doubt the supreme power that moves the universe. It is not possible to overstate that unique power as it reflects—like a kaleidoscope—many beautiful patterns on the Tree of Life, be it the spark of eros in the hidden Daath, or the profound compassion of charity illustrated in the fourth branch, or the divinely calm yet intense devotion and spiritual understanding emanated by the sixth. The kind of love residing in the seventh Tree branch is not easily controlled by its bearer. But its expression can be channeled, directed or aimed toward a chosen goal. (See Tree branch Number Eight.)

Within the qualities of the Tree of Life in its seventh branch, the force of maleness, inherent in branches Two and Four above, produces the *Hermaphrodite*, the bisexual offspring of the Greek deities Hermes and Aphrodite. As the lower arc of the horn of plenty (see Number Four), the sephirah Victory emphasizes once again the benevolent absence of limitations and the abundance of feelings.

Moreover, the Tree branch Number Seven (as does the numeral Seven) expresses the basic idea of perfection achieved through cyclic evolution. On an individual level, it can also mean the attainment of a personal realization. References to the "achieved completed seven" are found abundantly in many traditions over the globe, and in many human analogies in story and myth. In one of these, faithful Jews follow the Torah and observe the Sabbath as a day of active rest. It is to assimilate spiritual truth and to stay in line with the Lord God who, after having created the world in six days, rested on the seventh.

The "seven sacred qualities" of the Zoroastrian Ahura Mazda constitute a complete universe. In the Zend Avesta the earth is divided into seven parts with seven rivers. In the Christian's Lord's Prayer we find seven petitions (Figure 8), and the seven deadly sins: pride, anger, lust, gluttony, envy, covetousness and sloth.

Far East traditions account for seven human senses by adding the psychic perception of color and the spiritual understanding of sound to the Western five. The Hindus know seven yogas: raja, gnana, karma, bhakti, hatha, tantra (kundalini) and kriya.

In academic circles, a sabbatical year signifies a vacation after six years of teaching.

Figure 8. The Lord's Prayer
(Matthew 6:9-13)

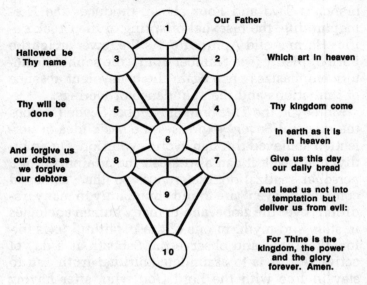

Our Father

1

Hallowed be
Thy name   **3**   **2**   Which art in heaven

Thy will be
done   **5**   **4**   Thy kingdom come

6

In earth as it is
in heaven

And forgive us
our debts as   **8**   **7**   Give us this day
we forgive   our daily bread
our debtors

9

And lead us not into
temptation but
deliver us from evil:

10   For Thine is the
kingdom, the power
and the glory
forever. Amen.

A few more words about the Number Seven. For Pythagoras, seven was the mystical composite of the spiritual three and the terrestrial four.

To Plato, seven was "God's beloved number." It is not surprising therefore that his platonic love ascended in seven definite modes from the purely personal to an impersonal emotion.

Victory is represented by the Olympic laurel wreath, and by all national flags and banners.

The planet Venus abides in this Tree branch, the goddess of love and beauty and one of the twelve Olympians.

The symbolic color vibration of Netzach is emerald green, that soothing color which lavishly covers nature's meadows and trees in summer. The seven-pointed star is its geometric figure. The Menorah or seven-branched candlestick (it was of solid gold in the Tabernacle of Moses, as described in Exodus 25:31) is its widely known symbol of illumination which was bestowed by the spirit of God (Figure 11).

The divine name and cosmic sound is Jehovah Tzabaoth, the Lord of Hosts.

AN OVERVIEW

Seventh Branch: The Number Seven

Title:
  Victory
  Netzach in Hebrew

Cosmic Sound:
  God-Name: Jehovah Tzabaoth
  Meaning: The Lord of Hosts

Figure Symbol:
  Seven-branched Candlestick (Menorah)

Planetary Sphere: Venus

Chemical Element/Metal: Copper

Position in:
  the Three Trinities: Astral or Magical
  the Three Pillars: Foot of Mercy
  the Four Worlds: Formation
                    Yetzirah in Hebrew

Celestial Hierarchies:
  Archangel: Auriel (Uriel or Haniel), The Grace of
  God
  Order of Angels: Elohim (The Divine Ones)
  Pseudo Dionysian (Christian): Principalities

Symbolic Colors in the World of —
  Origination: Amber
  Creation: Emerald-green
  Formation: Bright yellow green
  Manifestation: Olive flecked with gold

THE NUMBER EIGHT: Glory in Splendor
Hod in Hebrew

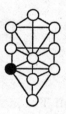

The Text:
  "The eighth path is called the Perfect and Absolute
Intelligence. The preparation of principles emanates
therefrom. The roots to which it adheres are in the
depths of the Sphere Magnificence, from the very
substance of which it emanates."

Be the master of your mind; it is yours not you!
  The eighth branch of the Tree of Life is the Number
Eight. Its name is Glory in Splendor. As the denser
arc of severe judgment in Number Five, and by growing side by side with strong emotions in Number

Seven, this sephirah has much opposition to overcome. To prevent unbridled feelings from making life become its own fool, fast and lively mind power emanates. And in manifold guise it carries mountains of dispassionate thoughts and intelligent ideas. With the ability to compare and conclude logically, the discriminating intellect leads to clear analytical thinking and practical constructive conclusions.

The sephirah Hod is the residence of the swift moving planet Mercury, whose name is derived from the chemical element Mercury. (The Greek Olympian Hermes and the Roman god Mercury are mythologically the same personage with frequently interchanged names. By analogy there is also a metaphysical identity with Hermes Trismegistus, the Egyptian Thoth and father of the great Hermetic rule.) Mercury is the messenger between God and humankind. The wings on his shoes quicken his mind and make him the lord of books and learning. His gift of memory—and sometimes of inspiration—lends him the power to search in the mental archives of the universe. Mercury's staff, called Caduceus, and made of entwined black-and-white twin serpents, heralds more forthcoming splits into duality. Once again, it reflects the ambivalent mind, its conscious and subconscious states, its waking thoughts and imaginative dreams.

Individually and collectively, Mercury and his staff illustrate the stage of the intersexual Androgyne (a parallel to the Hermaphrodite of Number Seven), which manifests the traits of both sexes. The Caduceus also points to humanity's constant battle between passion and reason, between ambition and doubt, between desire and logic. It refers to its bearer's own proverbial saying (the Hermetic rule), "As it is above, so it is below."

This Tree branch bears witness to Jean Jacques Rousseau's concept that "whatever we think, we are." And it also symbolizes Philo's view that "man's ability to reason is his defensive armor."

Though not obvious at first, the eighth branch of the Tree of Life points to the Eightfold Path of Gautama the Buddha, which guides humanitarian activities. This enlightened way serves as a clear plan for making friends with ourselves, just as the Bible commands "love thy neighbour as thyself" (Leviticus 19:18,34; Matthew 19:19, 22:39; Mark 12:31). For we must first truly accept ourselves before we can begin to contribute in any meaningful measure to the wellbeing of our neighbor and the human community at large.

The representative color of Hod is orange. Its chemical symbol is the mineral mercury, the quicksilver which escapes whenever one wants to catch it.

The divine name and cosmic sound is Elohim Tzabaoth, the God of Hosts.

The following chart compares the opposing qualities of the two Functioning Principles of Creation.

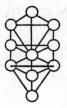

Branch Number Seven	*Branch Number Eight*
Victory/Firmness	Glory in Splendor
flood of feelings	mountains of thought
creative and formless	formative force
victory of emotions	glory of the mind
feelings look out for thoughts	thoughts look out for feelings
the urge to create	the urge to express
involuntary desires may blur instincts	conscious thoughts may clear the mind
creative imagination, intuition and inspiration	discrimination and pragmatic rationality
artists and dreamers	scientists and thinkers
the Lady of Love	The Lord of Books and Learning
the Hermaphrodite	the Androgyne

AN OVERVIEW

Eighth Branch: The Number Eight

Title:
    Glory in Splendor
    Hod in Hebrew

Cosmic Sound:
    God-Name: Elohim Tzabaoth
    Meaning: The God of Hosts

Figure Symbol:
    Caduceus

Planetary Sphere: Mercury

Chemical Element/Metal: Quicksilver

Position in:
    the Three Trinities: Astral or Magical
    the Three Pillars: Foot of Severity
    the Four Worlds: Formation
                         Yetzirah in Hebrew

Celestial Hierarchies:
    Archangel: Raphael, The Heavenly Physician
    Order of Angels: Beni-Elohim (Sons of God)
    Pseudo Dionysian (Christian): Archangels

Symbolic Colors in the World of:
    Origination: Violet purple
    Creation: Orange
    Formation: Russet-red
    Manifestation: Yellowish black flecked with white

THE NUMBER NINE: The Foundation
Yesod in Hebrew

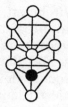

The Text:

"The ninth path is called the Purified Intelligence. It purifies the numerations, prevents and stays the fracture of their images, for it establishes their unity to preserve them from destruction and divisions by their union with itself."

Running around in circles and looking for stability.

Now the cosmic Lightning Flash turns vertical on its downward course, and with density rapidly increasing, the Number Nine emanates. Named *The Foundation*, it is that Tree branch which finishes the solid framework for the world of matter-to-be. Here everything is constantly turning and churning as if in a great hurry to assemble all generating powers into a uniform style to be ready in the tenth and last sephirah to "materialize."

This branch on the Tree of Life has many contradictory qualities, and its complex attributions are therefore more difficult to understand, particularly if this is your first encounter. According to numerous descriptive titles, the sephirah Foundation is at once the machinery of the universe, the vehicle of life, the purifier of emanations, the foundation of churches, the visible drapery around an invisible framework, the vision of independence, and the treasure house of images. It is also the seat of psychic life, the sphere of Maya, the abode of Hecate, and of the "Lady of Black and White Witchcraft," who can and often does lead humankind either to uncertain psychism or true intuition. Moreover, Yesod is the seat of automatic consciousness, and the home of the subconscious and the superconscious minds. It is likewise the abode of the goddess Diana, whose reproductive powers preside over childbirth. It provides the residence of the Aether of the Wise, that mysterious invisible fifth element (known as Akasha to the Hindus) which keeps the Four Elements of Life in balance.

There is still more to the ninth Tree branch. Levanah, the residing Moon, brings a pulsating flow from ebb to tide. It causes a ceaseless interchange between fluidity and solidity, and with it brings to the fore the basis for all "breathing life." Furthermore, this rhythmic motion divides infinity and timelessness into an essential measure of space and time. On the soon to materialize earth plane (the Number Ten), time in space will be needed. It cannot be otherwise. For the immensity of space can only be grasped by the moving rhythm of time; and vice versa, the moving of time can only be explored by its travel through space. As Plato remarked, "Time is the moving image of eternity."

There is a marked difference between the present and the now. The present is the rhythmic movement of time in space between the past and the future. The now is a timeless moment within a time that measures the present between past and future.

Another, and vitally important, split occurs in the sephirah Yesod. Allegorically, it is instigated by Cupid, the oldest of all gods, according to Hesiod, and the son of Venus and Mercury who (as you may recall) have their abode in the Tree branches Seven and Eight, respectively. Cupid divided every living thing into halves so as to make them whole again through "a union in love." This legend points to the actual gender split from the hermaphrodite (in Netzach) and androgyne (in Hod). With this split sexuality manifests as male and female, masculine and feminine. Libido comes into being, and with it the urge for creative reproductive sexual experience, now ready to join the already existing emotional and mental energies. Curiously, the reproductive powers are the very last to appear in the Great Plan of Life. But now, as the saying goes, "Sex is here to stay."

And that is not all that is happening in this Tree branch. For man's etheric and astral bodies appear, already longingly clinging to the physical matter-to-be in the next and last Tree branch. And there is, of course, also the Treasure House of Images which harbors psychological awareness. This "psychism" may confuse both one's genuine intuition and the clear thoughts that emanated in Netzach and Hod, respectively.

In fact, thinking and feeling may now easily run around in circles like a cat chasing its tail. To add to the confusion, there is one more duality experience in the offing in this sephirah. It is the vision of ultimate absolute Truth confronting relative truth which is experienced in terrestrial existence.

While in absolute reality Truth does not change, our relative truth does. For an infant, "mother" means security. For an adolescent, "mother" might mean unwanted apron strings. For an adult, "mother" means the natural birth-giver. To a philosopher, "mother" means one part of natural law. To the mystic, "mother" means the actual manifestation of the creating universal essence.

By analogy, Yesod is the Ark of Noah and the Holy Tabernacle found in churches and temples around the world. It is Atlas the Titan, on whose shoulders the world with all its heaviness rests. In Greek mythology this Tree branch represents numerous phallic gods, with Zeus, Jupiter, Jove and Pan leading the many.

The symbolic color vibration is purple, the noble favorite among high-ranking clergy in church hierarchies. The symbolic mineral is the weighty quartz and its beautifully shaped crystals.

The divine name and cosmic sound is Shaddai El Chai, The Almighty Living One God.

AN OVERVIEW

Ninth Branch: The Number Nine

Title:
The Foundation
Yesod in Hebrew

Cosmic Sound:
God-Name: Shaddai El Chai
Meaning: The Almighty Living One God

Figure Symbol:
The Altar

Planetary Sphere: Levanah (the Moon)

Chemical Element/Metal: Quartz (Crystal)

Position in:
the Three Trinities: Astral or Magical - Capston
the Three Pillars: Lower Part of Mildness
the Four Worlds: Formation
Yetzirah in Hebrew

Celestial Hierarchies:
Archangel: Gabriel, God is My Strength
Order of Angels: Cherubim (The Strong)
Pseudo Dionysian (Christian): Angels

Symbolic Colors in the World of:
Origination: Indigo
Creation: Purple
Formation: Very dark purple
Manifestation: Citrine flecked with azure

THE NUMBER TEN: "The Kingdom"
Malkuth in Hebrew

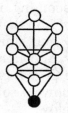

The Text:
"The tenth path is called Resplendent Intelligence, because it is exalted above every head and has its seat in Binah; it enlightens the fire of all lights and emanates the power of the principle of forms."

Let there be Life . . . in The Kingdom! It is the Number Ten and the last Tree branch, the planet Earth. While in Number Nine everything had seemed to be spinning around in circles, in Number Ten everything is where it belongs. Finally, the primal cause has reached its last effect in the totality of life, nature and humanity. With an inherent urge for stability, unity and harmony, the countless forms of finite matter are as one. The unfolding universe of matter is perpetually changing amidst stars we call planets, roaming around in the turning wheel of space we call the zodiac. Time measures the beginning and ending of all physical form, and points its finger at the union of differences.

Here in the phenomenal world of opposites and contradictions, the reality of absolute truth seems relative. Women and men are responsible for nature, its upkeep and its healthful growth. They are the workers of change in this temporal world of cause and effect where matter and form cannot exist without balance. Their actions and sensory expression create ever new beginnings and endings in procreation and reproduction.

The Number Ten is the World of Need, and ever receives without becoming more. It is the only branch on the Tree of Life that receives and absorbs all its powers solely and constantly from the nine branches above. This, of course, is just the reverse of Number One; for the Crown is the only Tree branch that gives all of its powers solely and constantly to the nine branches below.

In this, the last Tree branch, everything is interrelated and interdependent within the framework of the Four Elements of Life. Here, the powers inherent in Fire, Water and Air actually blend with dust to form the fourth element Earth. It is only fitting, therefore, and no coincidence that our planet bears the name of the Element which brought it forth.

Humankind is totally dependent on the presence of the Four Elements. Without Fire (as both light and warmth) we simply could not be. Without Air we would stop breathing. Without Water we could not survive. And without these three we could not till the soil. Later chapters contain more information concerning the Four Elements of Life.

The last Tree branch is rightly called the Kingdom. It is the Kingdom of Life. And yet, as it is said in *The Gospel According to Thomas*, "the kingdom of the father is spread upon the Earth, and men do not see it." It is true that we do not see it this way. To the contrary, we often call our Kingdom the Gate of Hell, Despair and Death, the Valley of Sorrow and Tears, and the "other side of the Garden of Eden."

These four colors are mixtures of previous Tree branch colors. The citrine color, corresponding to the element Fire, is a mixture of the green of branch Number Seven and the orange in branch Number Eight. The olive green, corresponding to Water, is a blend of the green in branch Number Seven and the purple in Number Nine. The orange in branch Number Eight and the purple in Number Nine mix into the color russet, corresponding to the element Air. And all colors in the branches Number One through Nine blend into black to correspond with the element Earth.

Malkuth is also the world of Shells and of Waste above the Qliphoth. The latter is the world of averse, evil and unbalanced forces—the world of anti-mat-

ter. This world of darkness and destruction is called
Hell in Christianity and the Underworld in Greek
mythology. The true mystic acknowledges the Qliphoth as the nether world but does not dwell on its
existence. He lights a candle instead of cursing the
darkness.

The Kingdom of Malkuth has many attributions.
As "Virgin Earth" it symbolizes the Bride awaiting
the King to become his Queen in the Kingdom. Sometimes this sephirah is named the "Inferior Mother,"
which signifies a reflection of the Eternal Mother in
Number Three. Called "the Footstool of God" and
"the Great Magnet," this last branch of the Tree of
Life is—kabbalistically expressed—the universal expression of wholeness.

Number Ten is of special significance to the mystic. With the tenth Tree branch, as we shall find in
the next chapter, the decad of numbers confirms that
numbers One and Ten are actually alike. "As above
so below . . . the One is in the Ten, and the Ten are in
the One." For by natural addition Number Ten (read
$10 = 1 + 0 = 1$) is twin to Number One, just as "the
Crown" (Number One) and "the Great Beyond" (the
infinite zero) read as $1 + 0 = 1$. And—most importantly—this is why You are an indispensable part of
it! As said before, You and the cosmos are one. Without You the universe would be wanting.

The Tree branch of Earth and the physical planet
Earth share the ancient symbol of the Solar Cross
which is the Cross of Nature with its four great elements in harmony. It is said that this equal-armed
cross is the origin of all later crosses, such as the

Christian Calvary Cross, the Buddhist Wheel of Life, the Egyptian Ankh and the Hindu Swastika. The latter is also one of the symbols of the Tree branch Kether.

With the Four Elements of Life in residence, the last Tree branch has four symbolic color vibrations: citrine, olive, russet and black. Its symbolic element is the clay of Earth. Its mineral is ever abundant salt, which is, again, a compound of two opposing parts, an acid and an alkali. When the Lord God said to the children of Israel, "You are the salt of the earth," it meant that they were capable of achieving harmony within all perpetually conflicting opposites.

Because of the differentiation that occurs between humans and nature, Malkuth, the Kingdom, has two cosmic sounds and divine names: Adonai Malekh, the Lord and King, and Adonai Ha Aretz, the Lord Made Manifest in Nature.

AN OVERVIEW

Tenth Branch: The Number Ten

Title:
   "The Kingdom"
   Malkuth in Hebrew

Cosmic Sound:
   God-Name: Adonai Malekh, Adonai Ha Aretz
   Meaning: The Lord and King,
            The Lord Made Manifest in Nature

Figure Symbol:
  Equal-armed Cross, Sandals, Double Cube

Planetary Sphere: The Elements, the Planetary
  Powers

Chemical Element/Metal: Salt, Earth

Position in:
  the Three Trinities: —
  the Three Pillars: Foot of Mildness
  the Four Worlds: Manifestation, Matter, Action
　　　　　　　　　　　Assiah in Hebrew

Celestial Hierarchies:
  Archangel: Sandalphon, The Messiah
  Order of Angels: Ashim (Souls of Fire) and
    Saintly Men on Earth
  Pseudo Dionysian (Christian): "Lovers of God"

Symbolic Colors in the World of:
  Origination: Yellow
  Creation: Citrine, olive, russet and black
  Formation: Citrine, olive, russet and black flecked
    with gold
  Manifestation: Black rayed with yellow

Summary:
  "Any thing is real only when it can be applied or
used for a purpose. For what good is the sun without
an Earth to shine upon, what good is a bird's song
when there is no ear to hear it, or what good is the
fragrance of a flower with no one to smell it?" My
Teacher expressed these thoughts quite frequently
and usually in a tone of great urgency. Let us pause

for a moment, therefore, and apply the reality of these words to the Tree of Life's wisdom.

With ten fully grown branches, the Tree of Life displays its reason for being: One has become the many and is pervading the whole. Much has happened on the way. The harmony of the Decad has been established in the created cosmos. The mobility in the first nine Tree branches has given way to a self-regulating stability in the tenth. The undifferentiated unity of oneness has ended in the harmony of multiplicity . . . opposites have met opposites and made way for action, unfoldment and progress . . . one radiant Light has become manifold Life . . . infinite life-force has scattered itself into myriads of forms as finite matter . . . the eternal has become temporal with its beginnings and its endings . . . the Crown, the mysterious gift from the Great Beyond, has found its King; together they have established their Kingdom in the Four Elements. On our planet Earth an invisible Unmanifest is visibly manifest as Humankind and Nature. In the solidity of terrestrial matter as the vessel for all that is perishable, all living things respond to friction; they feed and give off waste; they function and "work"; and they reproduce after their own kind.

In the Kingdom with its relative time and space—witnessed by the stars and the zodiac in the skies—the universe perceives and experiences the simple yet so sublime purpose of all creation.

And the purpose? It is *the human being, Infinity's end!* For we are the crowning glory of the Great Plan of Life and, by divine appointment, universal cocreators. It is therefore for us to *be* the faithful guardians of Nature, and heed her physical and spiritual laws. Nature's very own kingdoms of minerals, plants and animals need loving care. It is for us to plant and water all seeds and, later, to gather the harvest and share it with the needy.

The last branch of the Tree of Life is our home. While our life started on the last day of creation, we must now be the first to attend to our great privileges and terrestrial responsibilities. On the universal level, we thereby fulfill our life's fundamental reason and purpose.

III
More Patterns of Freedom

We have reached the central and largest part of the book. The Tree of Life, its separate and sacred paths, provide a kabbalistic framework which can now be compared with the revered tradition of several great metaphysical systems.

It becomes evident that the Tree of Life illustrates a universal concept when other transcendental systems are projected onto its branches. Each tradition takes a different vantage point and uses symbols different from those of the Tree of Life. These differences give additional clues regarding the basic character of the Tree, and amplify its various parts. Yet they *all* strive to reach the same goal: the Oneness of Life. Among these traditions are the Vedic trinity, the Four Elements of Life, the good versus evil battle of Zoroaster, the Chinese Tao of Lao-Tzu, the Law of Correspondence of Hermes Trismegistus, the Babylonian science of astrology, the Pythagorean number alphabet, and the Celestial Hierarchies.

The late Dr. Gershom G. Scholem, an authority on Jewish mysticism, remarked, "The Kabbalah, in its historical significance, can be defined as the product of the interpenetration of Jewish mysticism and Neoplatonism."

6

The Universe in Number

"The world is built by numbers manifest in form."
Thus said Pythagoras, genius of antiquity and teacher of numbers.[9] To that great sage (and equally applicable to the Tree of Life) the numbers from one to ten were the foundation of all creation and the purest form of science. Numbers were externalized forms and signs which revealed the secret bonds between the universe and humanity. Numbers illustrated the same harmonious relationships in the forces of gravity, in chemical affinities, in musical tones and in traveling stars. The decad set the cosmic stage on which life displayed the divine law and order of its inner realities. Though unchanged for 2,500 years to this day, the prestigious Pythagorean numbers have become robot-like automatic digits in today's industrialized world.

Long before Pythagoras gave his ideas on numbers to the world, numbers were "sacred currency," handled with genuine reverence as a cherished tradition. In those days, the science of numbers was part

of the Wisdom Religion observed by Hermes Trismegistus in Egypt, by Zoroaster in Persia, and by the
Holy Rishis in India. Moreover, numbers served as
potent tools to "know thyself" and were used in special forms of initiation; they were cosmic quality-
principles within the Laws of Life and not arbitrarily
chosen measures for tangible quantities.

In logical order, the measure of every number was
(and still is) exactly one half the sum total of its
preceding and its succeeding numbers. Thus, the
number two is half $1 + 3 = 4$; the number three is
half $2 + 4 = 6$; the number four is half $3 + 5 = 8$; the
number five is half $4 + 6 = 10$, and so on.

All Pythagorean numbers were considered offshoots of the number one, and proportional to one
another in a chain of alternating odd and even numbers. Odd numbers were considered to be divine, and
even numbers terrestrial. (Similarly, in the I Ching,
Yang refers to odd and Yin to even numbers.) Even
numbers were considered to be female because their
duality "divided and multiplied," such as $4 = 2 + 2$;
$6 = 3 + 3$; $4 \times 2 = 8$; and so on. Odd numbers were
male because they always had "the unity of the godhead in their midst," such as: $5 = 2 + 1 + 2$; $7 = 3
+ 1 + 3$; $9 = 4 + 1 + 4$.

Four numbers were "perfect," evidently in part because of their prominence in astrology: three for divine completion, seven for completed cyclic evolution, ten for completed harmony, and twelve for
government completed in perfection.

The numbers from one to nine were single or primary numbers. Consecutive numerals were compound numbers and mere repetitions of the first
nine, because they could be reduced to primary numerals by "natural addition" from left to right.

Numbers of distinct geometrical shapes were cred-
ited with an especial personality, and able to impart

their spatial character. For example, three, the triangle's three straight lines embody the "goal of every soul" and the three aspects of the mystical trinity; or four, the square or cube personifies "God manifest in form," and the cosmic evolution in matter. It is not surprising, therefore, that Plato proclaimed that "God geometrizes the universe and fashions it by numbers." You will find the Pythagorean shapes of the numbers from one to ten illustrated in Figure 9.

Figure 9. The Symbolic Shapes of Numbers According to Pythagoras

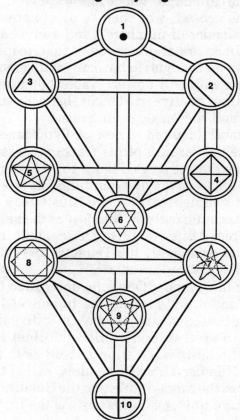

To continue the story of Pythagoras: after his initiation into the science of numbers by the high priests of Memphis, Thebes and Babylon, he continued and deepened his studies. By genuine intuition, he perceived more and more parallels and correspondences everywhere in the universe. While words could no longer express these fascinating relationships, mathematical digits and solid geometrical figures and numbers did carry their messages quickly and clearly. Pythagoras also believed that certain stars moved so rapidly that they emitted sounds which he called the "music of the spheres." The universe, he sensed, was thus "a symphony of sound and a calendar of numbers"; and a human being "a three-dimensional instrument that responded to melody with thought, to harmony with emotion, and to rhythm with will-power." Table 2 pictures the corresponding relative distances between the seven planets and the musical intervals.

The most inspired vision of Pythagoras and the fundamental essence of his teachings was and will always be the Tetractys (Figure 10). This equal-sided triangle encloses the first four numbers (1 + 2 + 3 + 4) in ten symmetrical dots and illustrates a unity in a fourfold cosmic pattern. And just as the ten branches of the Tree of Life are the numerical building blocks of the universe, so is the Tetractys the image of its fourfold cause and essence.

There the Number One (one dot, called the point) is the "odd-even" Monad, the impersonal omnipotent Godhead, and the symbol of indivisible unity. Number Two (two dots, called the line) represents manifest duality in creation as well as in transitory matter. Number Three (three dots, called the plane) illustrates the Monad linked to the Duad, and reveals the basis of universal harmony. As the first "harmo-

Table 2

THE PYTHAGOREAN "MUSIC OF THE SPHERES"

Geocentric View of the Seven Planets and the Musical Intervals

Planet	Moon	Mercury	Venus	Sun	Mars	Jupiter	Saturn
		Minor Scale				Major Scale	
Periodic Orbit (approx.)	28 days	12 weeks	2/3 year (3 Mercury orbits)	—	2 years (3 Venus orbits)	12 years	28 years
Tone	D	E	A	leading tone B or H	C	G	F

**Figure 10. The Pythagorean Tetractys
("The Sacred Triangle")**

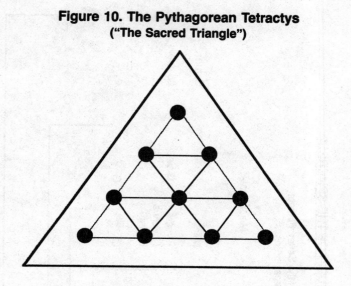

nious shape," the Triad symbolizes the phenomenal world hidden in the three-dimensional unity of both: *time* (duration: past, present and future) and *space* (distance: length, width and height). The Number Four (four dots, called the solid) symbolizes the Tetrad as the first "shape of perfection" in the evolution of matter.

Geometrically, the Decad presents the point, the line, the plane, the solid cube or pyramid (symbol of the universe).

Significantly, the ten-dot Tetractys convinced Pythagoras that the solar system must likewise en-

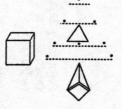

compass ten celestial bodies besides the Earth, not only the seven known in his day (Saturn, Jupiter, Mars, Sun, Venus, Mercury and Moon). Yet it took over two millennia to prove him right; for only within the last two hundred years were the missing planets (Uranus, Neptune and Pluto) discovered.

Because of *The Book of Formation*'s strong emphasis on numbers, let us look at the close kinship between the Pythagorean Decad and the Tree of Life.

The *Number One* of Pythagoras is the Noble Number. As the unchanging source of all numbers, it marks the beginning of creation; yet One is a number only if another number follows it. The One symbolizes indivisible unity beyond fatherhood and motherhood. It is also the number of Adam Kadmon, the perfected human. And it is no coincidence that both Roman and Arabic numerals draw the Number One in the straight standing figure of a man.

On the Tree of Life, Number One is the Crown of creation-to-be. It is the perpetual cosmic seed, the endless beginning in absolute unity. It is the "I Am That I Am," the Spirit of the Living God, the One Without a Second, the Monad.

The *Number Two* of Pythagoras is named the Bound. In contrast to the eternal unity of the One, Two signifies the transitory, the beginning of division, opposition and discord. It illustrates the imperfect state of humankind when breaking away from the Monad. Its symbolic two arrows pull in different directions, indicating the disharmony inherent in duality.

Number Two is the first number that can be multiplied by itself. Thereby it expresses the twofold struggle and goal of human life: to conquer the visible world with the help of the mind and five senses; and to reach the invisible "higher grounds" with the intuition, feelings and dreams. In Zoroaster's religious battle, the dual struggle was a discord between the "good light" of Ormuzd and the opposing "evil darkness" of Ahriman; yet nonetheless it was the darkness that allowed light to be seen.

In any event, Number Two was certainly no personal favorite of Pythagoras. It is said that he almost despised this number.

As a fascinating aside, and unbeknown to many, Number Two commemorates two seemingly unconnected events—one heathen and one Christian—in different guise on the same day. First is the pagan ritual of the ancient Romans who, partly from fear and superstition, paid homage to the Lord of the Underworld, Pluto. It happened on the second day of the second month after the second equinox, which was precisely the second day of November according to the Roman calendar of that time. This very day has survived in Christian calendars throughout the centuries as the mournful All Souls' Day.

On the Tree of Life Number Two means Wisdom. It is the mirrored reflection of the Crown's divine unity. In addition, it represents active male energy which—though eternally linked to the Godhead—is eagerly pursuing another direction to reach its own fulfillment in the all-receptive womb-man energy.

The *Number Three* of Pythagoras is the first truly odd number, the first perfect number (other than unity) and also the first of a geometric shape. It is the basic frame and great mystery of all creation. As already mentioned, the triad is composed of three straight lines; and thus it signifies divine completeness, and the unity behind all duality. Pythagoras believed that the three worlds, namely the natural, the human and the divine, sustain the balance of the entire universe.

This trinity-in-unity, as embodied in the Number Three, is found abundantly evident in sacred scriptures, in classical mythology, and even in Greek art and architecture. Here are a few examples. The Christian Bible has two distinct parts: the New Testament and Revelation, which together with the Old Testament form a trinity. The Old Testament itself is a triad: the books of Law, Prophets and Psalms. And so is the New Testament with its Gospels, Epistles and Revelation. The gifts of the Three Magi to the infant Jesus signify a cosmic threeness: Caspar's gold for God's wisdom, Melchior's frankincense for virtue, and Balthazar's myrrh for everlasting life. The trinity is also illustrated in the threefold mission of the Rabbi of Galilee: to preach the Word, to demonstrate signs and wonders and to go from death to resurrection.

In most world religions the Godhead is one in essence but a cosmic trinity in manifest parts: Father, Son and Holy Ghost for Christians, the Trimurti (three faces) of Agni, Vayu and Surya (fire, air and the sun) in the Vedas, and Nara, Nari and Viray (father, mother and son) in the Brahmanic tradition. In the more modern Hindu trinity of Brahma, Vishnu and Shiva, Brahma is the creator, Vishnu is the sustainer and Shiva symbolizes the Law of Change rather than permanent destruction. Ancient Egypt's triad of Osiris, Isis and Horus is symbolic of the sun, moon and earth trinity. In the Far East the Atma, Buddhi and Manas are known as the three fires of the soul. And in Greek mythology we find three-headed Cerberus, the three Graces, the three Furies and the three Fates. At Delphi, the oracle prophesied while seated on a tripod.

On the Tree of Life the Number Three means Understanding, eternal motherness and the bearer of new life. It is the universal cup of womb-man-hood. Its perpetual link with both the Godhead and the eternal male completes the divine triad. Expressed in numerals it reads: $1 + 2 = 3$ and also $3 = 1 + 2$.

The Tree of Life itself is a triple, a trinity.

The Number Four of Pythagoras is the tetrad. It is the symbol of evolution in matter, of cosmic formation, and of creation in action. It is also the first easily divided number because its numerals read $2 \times 2 = 4$ and $4 - 2 = 2$. It symbolizes the cosmos in divine repose, stability, and material fullness. Four is the first square, named the sacred square, and the first geometrical solids having a volume—the cube and the pyramid. As a symbol of immortality, the cube became the model for the altar in temple tabernacles.

There are countless expressions of the Number Four in the metaphysical as well as the physical world. In the holy scriptures, God finished the two great lights on the face of the earth on the fourth day (Genesis 1:14-19). Wise men of old counted Four Elements of Life: Fire, Water, Air and Earth. Aristotle distinguished four human temperaments: choleric, sanguinic, phlegmatic and melancholic. Gautama the Buddha spoke of the Four Noble Truths through which Nirvana (supreme inner freedom) is reached.[10] Ancient India knew a four-caste system, with a person's life divided into four basic stages.

Paracelsus, the fifteenth century alchemist and physician, ascribed great powers to the Four Elementals, each in its own Element: salamanders in Fire, undines in Water, sylphs in the Air and gnomes on Earth.

The Moon has four quarter-cycles. Human life has four stages: infancy, youth, adulthood and old age. The heart has four chambers. The human being is fourfold; a spirit with a soul, a mind and a body.

The planet Earth is four-square with an imaginary circumferential line running from north to south which intersects the equator (running East and West) at right angles. Legend tells us that these four cardinal points on the navigator's compass are guarded by four archangels who direct all ships on the high seas safely to their destination.

On the Tree of Life, Number Four illustrates the solid framework of creation-in-formation. It is the universal horn of plenty of the loving father and righteous ruler who shares his great wealth with true empathy, generously and gracefully yet indiscriminately, with all his people.

The Tree of Life itself is representative of four worlds (origination, creation, formation and manifestation), which embrace the four Hebrew letters of the ineffable name of the Lord God, YHVH.

The *Number Five* of Pythagoras has several meanings. Composed of a duality and a triad, it brings order into the disorder caused by an overabundance of Tree branch Number Four. It is at once the number of justice and destiny, and the number of humanity. Its form is the Pentagram. Because of its symbolic ties to the hands and feet (the tools of activity) it is the historic emblem of the Olympic Games as well as of Pythagorean philosophy.

As a symbol of good and evil, Number Five points to friction and confusion, either now or in the future. It is not so bad, since by choosing between the good or evil, we gain our independence and freedom.

In Plato's *Timaeus*, a kinship is shown to exist between five regular solid figures (called the sacred Platonic "volumes") and the five universal elements. These are the hexahedron or cube, symbolic of Earth; the icosahedron, symbolic of Water; the octahedron, symbolic of Air; the tetrahedron symbolic of Fire; and the dodecahedron, symbolic of a fifth Element, Ether, the celestial sphere of spirit. This last solid figure contains five hexahedrons, one for each of the Elements—Fire, Water, Air, Earth and Ether.

By analogy, the stars (planets) wandering in the skies (zodiac) form five major relationships (aspects) which rhythmically recur: the conjunction (σ), sextile ($\times$), square ($\square$), trine ($\triangle$), and opposition (σ^{Q}).

In the Hebrew mysteries, the five-pointed star expresses God's will for humankind. For example, the star personifies the five component parts of the body: the head and four limbs. It also reflects the five senses which protect one in the jungle of earthly existence: sight, sound, smell, taste and touch.

There is more. With five fingers on each hand and five toes on each foot, a covenant was made between the Lord God and the patriarch Abraham (Genesis, Chapter 17). Five sacrifices were demanded of Abraham (Genesis 15:9). The Torah consists of the five books of Moses. Five wounds were inflicted on the Nazarene during his crucifixion. The world of Islam is built on five pillars. Most significantly, however, the Pentagram shape itself represents the mortal yet evolving human being, represented by a man, with his feet apart and arms outstretched. As mentioned earlier, the Pentagram (Figure 5) is the only geometric shape able to move in two opposing directions: it can be either an expansion or a contraction.

On the Tree of Life, the Number Five is the number of Severity, Justice and Destiny, as well as the sacrificial priest-warrior and the cosmic surgeon. Its awesome strength is all too often misunderstood. Five is the weigher of good and evil, and also represents the Lipikas (scribes of Karma) in Eastern philosophy. It is the universal law of cause and effect in action, which defends and protects what is right and succeeds through perseverance and strength.

The Number Six of Pythagoras expresses balance and harmony, also reciprocity and interchange. It signifies the perfection of parts, because it is the only number under ten which divides into a double "harmonious three." This double triad illustrates the creative intermingling of spirit and matter (God and human) in balanced harmony.

Its geometrical symbol, the Hexagram, figures the equal measure of both the threefold divine power pervading created matter, and the terrestrial human reaching toward the triune god. Mindful that the world was created in six days (Exodus 20:11), the six-pointed star is the Shield of David, the emblem of the state of Israel, and the sign of the Hindu Creator God, Vishnu. The Hexagram is also the cosmic pattern of all snowflakes; no two have ever been found to be exactly alike.

The Number Six is the basis of various measurements. For instance, the space within the Great Pyramid was measured by multiples of six. Since early times, days have been measured as 24 (4 x 6) hours; hours gauged as 60 (6 x 10) minutes; and minutes metered as 60 (6 x 10) seconds.

On the Tree of Life the Number Six is the heart of the Tree in its harmony and beauty. It symbolizes the six dimensions in space which the Lord God sealed to His holy name, namely: east, west, north, south, height and depth of all matter (Figure 27).

Six also discloses the turning point where divine force starts to assume visible form, and where mortal humanity begins to manifest divinity. Remember, it is here that the Son of God became the Son of Man, and that the ascending Son of Man became the Son of God.

The *Number Seven* of Pythagoras is another perfect number. As the sum total of Numbers Three and Four, it is primarily spiritual, but also earthy in nature. It signifies divine creativity, completion and transformation in cyclic evolution. In addition, it refers to time and its rhythmic motion. Its geometric shape is the seven-pointed star, the Heptagram.

There are over 1,500 references to the Number Seven in the Bible. After creation was finished in six days, God blessed the seventh, the Sabbath, as a day of rest. Jacob's famous ladder had seven rungs. Several religions count seven heavens. For ancient Egyptians, seven signified eternal life. The Persians had seven sacred horses. The Hindus had seven devas. And the Chaldeans had seven angels.

The allegorical meaning of Seven as a completed cycle is visible in many and altogether different ways. Seven in fairy tales and folklore, marks an everlasting happy ending after a chain of great obstacles. Seven circuits around the sacred Kaaba in Mecca complete a Muslim pilgrimage. Christians observe seven sacraments; the universe is ascribed with seven rays; and Buddha attained illumination during his seventh week under the Bodhi Tree. There are seven holy Rishis in the Vedas and seven Archangels in the book of Revelation. Seven planets light the firmament; the Hebrew mystics of old saw them as the "seven eyes of God." In ancient Greece, seven sages created seven sacred sciences for required study in the Pythagorean Academy, namely: arithmetic, astronomy, dialectic, geometry, grammar, music and rhetoric. The seven strings on the lyre of Orpheus corresponded to the sevenfold prismatic scales of light. In their musical intervals, the melodies from these strings were to bring the human soul into harmony with beauty and truth.

The sevenfold human body can be divided in four different ways: The body (head, chest, abdomen, two arms, and two legs); the organs (heart, liver, lungs, stomach, spleen, and two kidneys); the functions (respiration, circulation, assimilation, secretion, reproduction, sensation and reaction); and the "open windows" (mouth, two eyes, two ears and two nostrils).

To Plato, Seven was God's beloved number. His *Timaeus* states that the "soul of the world was created out of the Number Seven." And his universally famous "platonic love" was also of seven kinds.

As already mentioned, the Menorah or the seven-branched candle stand is probably the most venerat-

Figure 11. Menorah, Symbol of the Tree of Life

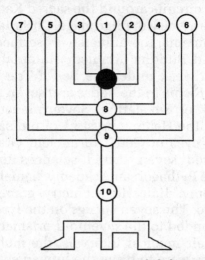

The seven-branched candelabrum is described in Exodus 25:31, 32. It was made for the Sanctuary in the wilderness, and later transferred to the Temple (I Kings 7:49).

ed symbol of the Number Seven (Figure 11). To be found in every Hebrew temple, synagogue, home of the devout, and in many Christian churches as well, it illustrates the divine order and harmony with a trinity on either side of the sacred Number One (3 + 1 + 3).

In relating to time and rhythm, the Number Seven is in many corners of terrestrial existence, such as the seven day week and the seven year cycles in the life of humankind.

On the Tree of Life the Number Seven signifies Victory achieved on many levels by way of the power of feelings. It is decidedly the realm of creative activity, of intuitive perception, and the sharing of a very special kind of love.

The *Number Eight* of Pythagoras refers to a termination of evolution, to regeneration and to perpetual spiral motion. It symbolizes justice, because it divides and separates naturally into two Fours, and then again into two Twos, and again into two Ones. As a double Four it represents solidified matter which must not be confused with the evolution of matter in the Number Four. The Number Eight is also the only "evenly even" cube number in the Decad and reads 2 x 2 x 2. Its geometric shape is the eight-pointed star and also the fused double square.

The bird of life, a traditional Hindu symbol, is a reflection of the Number Eight, for it carries humankind from the physical, the lower half of the eight (a), to higher grounds, the upper half of the eight (b). Moreover, when written horizontally, the Number Eight is the sign of infinity. When split in half vertically, it becomes two Three's looking at one another, as though through a mirror of the mind.

a　　　　　　b

Attributions to the Number Eight are numerous. In music, the octave is the eighth note counting from the first. It repeats the ground tone and terminates the musical scale upward or downward. In his Eight-Fold Path, Gautama Buddha taught the cessation of suffering. Dante's "eighth day of purgatory" symbolizes the return to unity.

The Jewish rite of male circumcision is performed on the eighth day after birth. On the eighth day after the deluge, eight saved souls left Noah's Ark. Baptismal fonts in Christian churches are always octagonal

Figure 12. Islamic Octagonal Design
(Sixteenth Century)

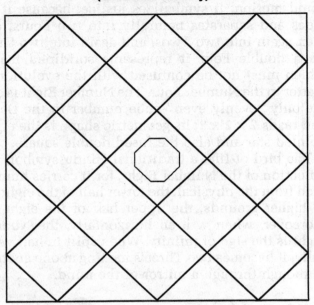

in design, illustrating the birth of new spiritual life. In mosques octagonal designs are found in great profusion (Figure 12).

On the Tree of Life, the Number Eight denotes Splendor and Glory. It relates to the thinking mind, which is able to remember and formulate thoughts, to balance desires, and even to dream. With Mercury (the messenger of the gods) in residence, his prominent double-serpent staff indicates existing ambiguous qualities.

The *Number Nine* of Pythagoras is the most difficult of all numbers to comprehend because of its many, and often contradictory, qualities. Called the

Concord, the Number Nine unites and knits together all primary numbers into a certain finality (1 + 2 + 3 + 4 + 5 + 6 + 7 + 8 + 9 = 45 and 4 + 5 = 9). Its geometrical shape is the nine-pointed star. It represents aspiration and judgment. It marks a termination, and yet the close attainment of a goal. It is another sacred number, the number of muses, the continual harmony of harmonies, and is also an angelic number dedicated to the Trinity.

As the trinity of trinities (3 x 3) the Number Nine illustrates divine perfection. As the Number Three multiplied by itself, it symbolizes the "marriage of the active and the passive" which perpetually balances and reproduces itself.

And yet, as the first square of an odd number, the Number Nine embodies baffling and frequently conflicting characteristics. It is at once double-edged and cyclic, angelic and despised. By many it is considered a "bad number with a ferocious appetite" because it is the only numeral in the Decad which reproduces itself incessantly. If Nine is multiplied by itself, or by any other single digit, its natural addition will always be again a nine: 9 x 9 = 81; and 8 + 1 = nine; 9 x 4 = 36; and 3 + 6 = 9; and so with any other digit. It is much the same as the awesome snake Hydra in Greek mythology, whose nine heads were perpetually cut off every day and grew back again overnight.

In a personal way, the Number Nine was to Pythagoras the "emblem of matter" and the reproductive power which can never be annihilated, even though its form changes continually. Therefore, he enthroned it in the 360-degree zodiacal wheel, because 3 + 6 + 0 in natural addition becomes a nine.

Arcane wisdom, tradition and philosophy give subtle clues to the meaning of this bewildering number. For example, the Eleusinian Mystery initiations were always conducted in nine-day periods. The Bible tells of nine blissful beatitudes and nine fatal woes. At the beginning of the first century, Apollonius of Tyana, a Greek philosopher and ardent Pythagorean, declared the ninth hour as the most suitable for meditation and prayer. To this day, Roman Catholics observe the Novena as their nine-day devotion to particular saints. For the medieval clergy the Number Nine was an extension to the Holy Trinity, and thereby the basis of their angelic orders—a subject of a later chapter. The Enneagram teachings of Gurdjieff attach special importance to the mythical and mysterious Number Nine.

On the Tree of Life the Number Nine marks the finale of formation. It represents the rhythmic foundation of unifying cyclic powers which are interconnecting prior to imminent physical manifestation. Two significant splits occur: one into the ebb and tide of time in space; and the other into male and female sexuality. The Number Nine relates also to an "automatic consciousness," and an enhanced harmony that is distinct from the balanced harmony of the Number Six.

The *Number Ten* of Pythagoras is a number of total harmony and fulfillment, and of manifestation completed in unity. It is the most perfect number of evolution as it contains all other numbers of the Decad. For the sum total of $1 + 2 + 3 + 4 + 5 + 6 + 7 + 8 + 9 + 10$ is 55; and 55 in natural addition $(5 + 5)$ is 10. It is likewise the union of the numbers $1 + 2 + 3 + 4$. Moreover, Ten is the fusion of the spirit, soul, mind and body, as well as the solidarity of the Four Elements of Life. The geometric shape of the Number Ten is the ten-pointed star.

To the disciples of Pythagoras, Ten was indeed a holy number. They swore by the ten sacred dots of their Tetractys, much the same as when the President of the United States and other elected governmental officials place their hand on the Bible when taking the oath of office.

All world systems of belief encompass the Number Ten, each in its own way. The ten princedoms in legendary Atlantis were ruled by ten priest kings (Plato). The Rig Vedas have ten books of hymns. Indra, the Vedic god of the firmament, has ten heads of enlightenment. There are ten oriental yogas (including the basic four). The enlightened Buddha possessed ten talents to understand the ten paths of Karma. Northern Buddhism knows of ten sublime virtues. The Bible lists Ten Commandments which for orthodox Jews rank higher than the Holy Torah. Ten was a prevalent measure to gauge space and distance in the temples of Solomon and Ezekiel. Since the days of the Pharisees, ten men complete the number required for temple worship. The traditional Ten Days of Penitence between the New Year and the Day of Atonement illustrate the Jewish people's burning desire to stay in tune with their Creator.

On the Tree of Life the Number Ten expresses the universe completed in living matter. With the Kingdom firmly established in the equal-armed cross, it harmonizes all Tree branches like the Decad of numbers unifies all digits. Yet in its deepest meaning, the Number Ten is the manifest One in the first Tree branch returning to the unmanifest Zero of the Great

Beyond. Again, in natural addition: the Number Ten
(1 + 0) links the One which created all to the Zero
from which it had emerged. In reality therefore, both
the ten branches on the Tree of Life and the Pythagorean Decad illustrate the ever new and constantly
revolving cycle of creation.

In summary, this is what Pythagoras told the world
with his sacred Decad: While walking on earth as the
Number One, neophytes step into duality in the
Number Two. By adding the Number Three, they become aware of triune harmony. With the following
Number Four the evolving souls are indeed able to
create and build in shapes and forms. By adding the
Number Five they learn to discriminate between
good and evil, and thus exercise free will. With the
Number Six and cosmic consciousness, seekers find
the harmony of love and beauty. With the Number
Seven they develop the power of feeling, and a grasp
of the forthcoming completion in rhythmic evolution. In the Number Eight they experience the fullness of that evolution with the help of their newly
found mind and memory. In the Number Nine—and
after a last struggle—they arrive at their solid foundation. In the Number Ten they are mindful of the eternal Laws of Life in divine perfection. Fully awake
and ever aware of their great birthright, souls are
finally able to magnify the glory of Life itself . . . a
truly genuine freedom!

My Teacher had his own, most unusual way of
looking at the ten branches of the Tree of Life. Here
are his own words.

"Numbers, as seen, written and used, are by themselves living principles. They are always the enve-
lopes for an inside letter which carries its own mes-

sage. In the chain of life, therefore, each letter becomes in turn the envelope of another letter, again with a message of its own. And so it goes throughout the numbers from One to Ten. Only the Number One (without a preceding letter) is both message and envelope. Its message heralds the primordial power which creates, contains and sustains the total universe. And the envelope of the Number One is in fact the envelope of, again, the total universe; without it there could not be any message.

"So it is with man! By being the Number One he is both message and envelope, and thereby the only creature on Earth who can stand and walk erect. The Number One is his treasure, his essence, his origin, and his home. The outside world is only the mirror-image of his own reality. His ten fingers till the soil on which his ten-toed feet walk.

"As envelope, the Number One holds a letter in its fold. It is the *wisdom* of the Number Two whose message tells of duality, of orderly-divided space, and of man's free-moving creative force. And as Two becomes the envelope of the Number Three, its inside letter of *understanding* carries the life-creating and quietly preserving form, along with man's great yearning for unity. As Three turns into the wrapper for the Number Four, its inside letter tells of the need for action. Through unselfish love and faith it affirms man's inherent benevolence, mercy and compassion. As Four envelops Number Five, the inside letter of Justice and Severity recounts the unbreakable Laws of Life. It urges man to fight for what is right, and to dispose voluntarily of what is unnecessary. When Five shifts into the envelope for the Number Six, the inside letter speaks of beauty and harmony. It invites man to pause for a little while and enjoy Beethoven's Sixth(!) Symphony, the Pastorale. While Six then en-

velops the Number Seven, the inside letter introduces the Victory of feelings. It kindles man's desire
for artistic expression, and for a more terrestrial love
in action. As Seven becomes the envelope for the
Number Eight, the inside letter is about Splendor and
Glory. It tells of man's kaleidoscopic mind, and his
discriminating thoughts about 'this and not that.'
And as Eight switches to the envelope for Number
Nine, the inside letter carries the Foundation. It men-
tions man's efforts to escape from 'running around in
circles' (as most people do); and it points to man's
vision of the good things to come.

"Yet personally," so my Teacher related, "Nine has
the most beautiful message of all numbers. As an
envelope, its powerful majesty makes way for ebb
and flow, for time and space, for male and female. Its
inside letter heralds the glorious birth of the Number
Ten, the Kingdom. And Ten (read 10 = 1 + 0) is the
only letter which never becomes an envelope. Instead it marks a new beginning for humankind . . . the
Number One of the manifest is meeting the Zero of
the yet unmanifest. Thus the rhythmic circle of life
starts over again with all its freshness and newness.
And its spiral motion will reach higher and higher
grounds, *always*. Such is the Story of Man."

While we are still on the subject of Numbers, let us
look for a moment beyond the Decad. There, the
numbers Eleven and Twelve in the spaces of the zodiac demand our attention and understanding in
preparation for forthcoming chapters on Kabbalistic
astrology.

Number Eleven, according to the Pythagoreans, is
difficult to confront because it is ambiguous in character. On the Tree of Life it marks two crucial midway

points. One is halfway between "the Godhead" of Number One and "the teacher" of Number Twenty-two. The other is between "the harmony" of Number Ten and "the perfected government in equilibrium" of Number Twelve.

In Christian tradition, the proverbial Eleventh Hour (Matthew 20:6, 9) is symbolic of harmony aiming toward perfection, yet falling short of it. Sometimes Eleven is also labelled the number of sin and transgression; especially since, after Judas' betrayal and the crucifixion of Jesus, the remaining eleven disciples of the Nazarene failed to establish the heralded Kingdom of God.

Kabbalistically, Number Eleven is considerably harder to contend with than Number Two. While Two leaves the undivided unity of One, Eleven departs from the established harmony of Ten. The Roman numerals reflect these subtle qualities and differences visually; they use equal strokes for Number Two (I and I), but unequal symbols for Number Eleven (X and I).

Number Twelve, to Pythagoras, was a "perfect" number, the harmonious result of Three as unity in essence, pluralized by Four as the state of manifest bodily existence ($12 = 3 \times 4$). It personified apostolic authority and equilibrium and the architecture of the universe perfected in sacred space.

Kabbalistically, Number Twelve represents cyclic completion in orderly divided space. It symbolizes the union of spirit and matter. In folklore, it heralds the marriage of heaven and earth.

In Greek mythology the twelve Titans were the first gods to govern the world from the Great Mount Olympus. The Twelve Labors of Hercules personified the severe probationary tests which—in the ancient Egyptian and Greek mystery schools—every aspiring neophyte had to pass before initiation. The Roman Empire inscribed its law in Twelve Tables. The Bible's Old Testament records an unbroken succession of twelve Patriarchs from Seth to Noah, and another dozen from Shem to Jacob. The twelve sons of Jacob, in turn, became the Twelve Tribes to govern Israel. Twelve Patriarchs presided over the early Christian Church. At that time, the breastplates of high priests were studded with twelve precious stones. The Nazarene was twelve years old when he first spoke in the temple about God's government (Luke 11:42); later he surrounded himself with twelve apostles. Francis of Assisi had twelve faithful brothers.

In his last discourse, Gautama Buddha mentioned his twelve disciples. Hindus have twelve Bodhisattvas (enlightened spiritual beings) as teachers. Twelve knights sat at King Arthur's Round Table. Most calendars count twelve months.

The book of Revelation tells of twelve open gates to enter the New Jerusalem. These open gates seem to symbolize the twelve senses of the allegorical Adam Kadmon, the perfected human being. For to reach the blissful state of freedom, humans need more than the protective five physical senses: hearing, sight, smell, taste and touch. One must also be guided by what can be called seven metaphysical senses: the awareness of living (duration), self-movement, balance, temperature (hot and cold), word-sense (speech), thought (as stored memory), and personality (ego).

Numbers was once the informal language of both the priest-kings of Atlantis and the learned priesthood of Egypt. Moses, and later the Nazarene, conversed in Numbers. Numbers are the crown jewels in the world of Pythagoras—the key to Plato's universe and the backbone to Aristotle's logic. Numbers are externalized relationships, and the mirror for Einstein's universe. Numbers are the language of science to this day.

And tomorrow? Numbers will tell the story of quasars, of weightless superclusters and of galaxies at ten billions of light-years' distance soaring away from tiny blue planet Earth into the Great Beyond, at a speed of close to 186,000 miles each second.

*. . . I have created him for
my glory; I have formed
him; yea I have made him.*
Isaiah 43:7

7

Four Faces of the World

As the Tree of Life emanates along the Path of the Lightning Flash, creation progresses in four successive steps, and does so with gradually increasing density from fine into coarse. This produces what is called the Four Worlds, not worlds in the usual sense of the word, but distinct metaphysical spheres of manifestation. Consider them to be different stages of cosmic evolution, and that each world sustains the next by its fundamental function and purpose.

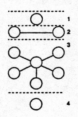

In their totality, the Four Worlds reveal how (1) radiant Light becomes vibrant Life; (2) infinite Spirit expresses itself as finite Matter; (3) the primal cause

119

of free-moving Force takes tangible form as its last effect; and (4) in the conceptual (not the chemical) sense, the Four Elements of Life manifest in matter and in humanity (Figure 13).

Technically, there are two ways of grouping the Four Worlds on the Tree of Life. One uses a single Tree, the other four connected Trees (Figures 14 and 15). According to the one-Tree version, the Creator conceives and emanates the plans in the first World, designs them in the second, forms and moves them in the third, and materializes them in the fourth. In the second version, with one full Tree in each of the Four Worlds, the last branch of the first Tree becomes

Figure 13. The Ways of the Four Worlds

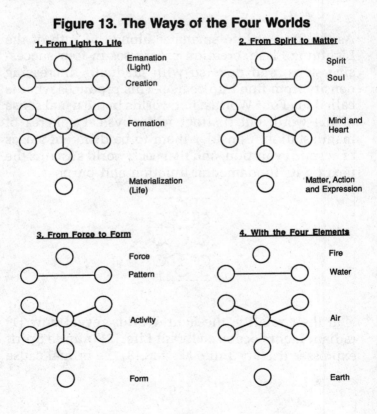

1. From Light to Life

- Emanation (Light)
- Creation
- Formation
- Materialization (Life)

2. From Spirit to Matter

- Spirit
- Soul
- Mind and Heart
- Matter, Action and Expression

3. From Force to Form

- Force
- Pattern
- Activity
- Form

4. With the Four Elements

- Fire
- Water
- Air
- Earth

Figure 14. The Four Worlds in Manifest Existence
(Version One)

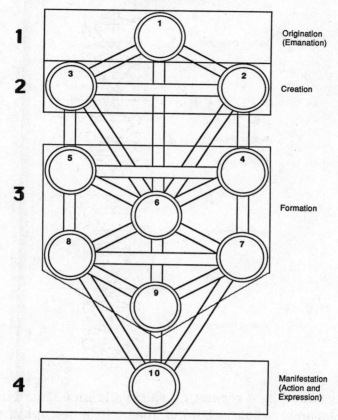

1 — Origination (Emanation)

2 — Creation

3 — Formation

4 — Manifestation (Action and Expression)

the first branch in the second; the last branch of the second Tree becomes the first branch in the third; and the last branch of the third Tree becomes the first branch in the fourth. Except for the Angelic Hierarchies, this book follows the single-Tree grouping of the Four Worlds.

Each one of the four consecutive worlds on the Tree of Life represents a different quality of expression or a different level of consciousness. Each is

Figure 15. The Four Worlds in Manifest Existence
(Version Two)

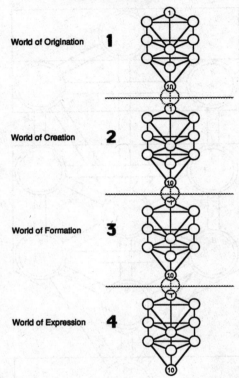

World of Origination **1**

World of Creation **2**

World of Formation **3**

World of Expression **4**

guarded by a separating veil. Veils hide, guard and separate what is behind them. In a metaphysical sense, veils herald a change in vibration and function as a partition to protect an abyss or a void. Of the seven veils on the Tree of Life, three are above the Tree in the Great Beyond, and four are between its branches. The three veils in the Great Beyond establish the triune unity needed for creation to start, and the four veils between the Tree branches express the solid framework of emanation leading to creation.

Of the Four Worlds, the first is the World of Origination or Emanation (Atziluth in Hebrew). As the home of only one Tree branch, the Crown, it is the plane of the all-pervading light of the Godhead, of pure existence in never-changing power, and the source of limitless life. Only in the first world does light come directly from the Great Beyond. The three successive worlds receive their light along the Path of the Lightning Flash and are, therefore, sometimes referred to as the "Garments of *that* Light," or "the Beautiful Garment of God." The veil of Kether partitions the Godhead in the first world from the nine Tree branches below, because, as Lord Krishna tells in the Bhagavad Gita, "I am in them, yet they are not in me."

Second is the World of Creation (Briah in Hebrew). It is the plane of awakened archetypal forces having two interacting Tree branches: Wisdom, the creatively expanding dynamic maleness, and Understanding, the receptive, life-bringing and preserving femaleness. The veil separating the World of Creation from the third World below points to a change from force to form and expression and hides the Tree branch Daath.

Third is the central World of Formation (Yetzirah in Hebrew) with six direction-giving Tree branches, namely: (1) the generous outpouring of Mercy; (2) the restricting and correcting Severity of Justice; (3) the balancing love of Beauty; (4) the firm Victory of feelings and instincts; (5) the splendid Glory of mind and thoughts; and (6) the Foundation for vibrant life with its newly evolved sexuality of male and female. There are two guarding veils in the World of Formation. The Veil of Paroketh separates the heart of the Tree of Life, Beauty the King, from the four creatively functioning branches below. The veil of Malkuth, the universal counterpart to the veil of Kether, conceals the Kingdom from the nine Tree branches above so as to "guard the fruit" of the Tree of Life.

Fourth is the phenomenal World of Manifestation in matter (Assiah in Hebrew). Having only one Tree branch, the Kingdom within its sphere is the plane of solid matter, of physical expression, of action, of creation and procreation. It is the crown of creation, the physical planet Earth. Sometimes named "the fruit of the Tree of Life," it is the world in the making, where human supremacy embraces the entire community of nature with its own "worlds": minerals, plants, animals and humankind itself. While solid minerals and mountains may show no independent movement, they are in a state of continual motion within, and by no means lifeless. The great Sufi Hazrat I. Khan said, "God slept in the mineral kingdom, dreamed in the vegetable world, and awoke in the kingdom of the animals, so that he could be very active in humankind."

To repeat, both the First and the Fourth Worlds hold only one single branch in their fold. "As above so is it below." The all-pervading spirit (in the first plane of existence) reflects itself in the crystallized spirit (in the fourth). Matter is dense spirit and spirit is fine matter.

Analogies to the Four Worlds are to be found literally everywhere in daily life. The birth of a child is an example in point. First, there is the desire to have a child. Next is the act of creation, the moment of conception through the union of man and woman. The following nine months of pregnancy form and build the child's body. And lastly, the arrival of the newborn infant is the physical expression of the initial intention.

Another practical parallel is the baking of a cake. First is the original intention to make a cake. To create it, a recipe is needed. To form the cake the ingredients are blended in proper order and the mixture is baked according to directions. Lastly, the cake is taken out of the oven ready to eat.

The Four Color Scales, classified by Aleister Crowley, apply to the Four Worlds on the Tree of Life. The colors for each branch are listed in the overview which follows the description of each Tree branch. Aristotle defined color as the result of active interplays between light and darkness. Thus transparent colors signify the World of Origination. Colors assigned to the Creative World symbolize reflected colors in nature. Colors which indicate the Formative World are a mixture of the first two scales. And a flecked mixture of the preceding three color schemes refers to the World of Manifestation.

On a metaphysical level, in relating the story of the Nazarene, the Four Gospels follow the framework of the Tree's Four Worlds. There, in the World of Origination, the evangelist John tells of the spirit of Christ. Luke illustrates the sacrificial love, the soul of Christ, that is in the World of Creation. Mark stresses the sublime powers inherent in the Son of God in the World of Formation. And Matthew, in the World of Manifestation, narrates the human story of Christ as the Son of Man. In the Old Testament (Ezekiel 1:5-10), the prophet's vision of four four-faced and four-winged living creatures refers to the Four Worlds in the appearance of the faces of a man, a lion, an ox and an eagle.

In the Zend Avesta we read about the Four Worlds in the steps of faithful seekers. The first step places

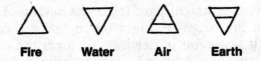

them in the good-thought paradise; the second step in the good-word paradise; the third step in the good-deed paradise; and the fourth step in the endless light.

The Four Elements of Life, Fire, Water, Air, and Earth, interlock totally with the Four Worlds in the Tree of Life. Known under various names as the Ancient Root Elements, Natural Elements, Elements of the World, or the Elements of the Wise, they surround us at all times and on every level of life. Down through the ages, they have always played a dominant role in the lives of peoples and cultures. To Pythagoras and Plato, they were natural forces sustained by the terrestrial manifestation of the Laws of Life. To the Persian Sufi poet Rumi (1207-1273), they were the Four Servants of God. To my Teacher they were the Four Faces of the Universe and the Four Architects of Nature. To all medieval alchemists, but particularly to the German physician Paracelsus (1493-1541), the Four Elements were the primal essence within all that can be felt and touched.

Mystics believe that the Elements permeate everything. In other words, the Four Elements of Life are not physical states (as our science knows them) but rather the living conditions in which all chemical elements exist and interact. In every cell of the human body they engage in the transcendence of matter. In fourfold interaction they provide the master key for the interpretation of astrology.

The Four Elements of Life are the chemicals of life itself, and also the forms of all they contain. Accordingly, the element Earth is solid Water, and the element Air is solidified Fire. These principles have

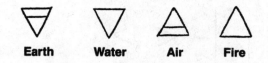

greater merit than a visual resemblance of their symbols would indicate; for both Water and Earth are cold and coarse, and both Fire and Air are hot and fine (Table 3).

Among their "physical" characteristics we find that Fire (both as visible flame and light or heat) ascends, expands and transforms. It is hot, radiant, dry and dynamic, as is the World of Origination. Water descends, purifies, condenses and dissolves to promote germination without manifesting itself in structured forms. It is cold, moist, receptive and absorbing, as is the World of Creation. In shape and color Water conforms with its receptacle. Air supports and dispenses. Being so finely divided that it cannot be seen, it scatters in all directions, and moves everything with it. It is hot, moist, expanding and adjusting, as is the World of Formation. Earth confines itself to touchable matter. It is cold, dry, brittle, receptive, passive, concreting, restricting, stable, inert and solid, as is the World of Manifestation (and, of course, the planet Earth). And yet like the carbon atom, Earth has fourfold skills to enter into varied relationships.

Physical science corresponds with the Four Elements of Life by differentiating the static (solid) Earth and the three mobile substances—gaseous Air, liquid Water, and the two-faced dynamic Fire (light and heat). The definition of Fire is a matter of semantics because alchemical Fire is that which makes all chemical matter burn when ignited. Is this not a perfect description of the Tree of Life's Godhead that permeates all that exists?

As citizens of Four Worlds, human beings are a

Table 3

THE FOUR ELEMENTS OF LIFE

Element	Symbol	Direction	Activity (+/-)	Color	Density	State	Relationships
Fire	△	upward	self- (+) expressive	bright	fine	mobile	△ boils ▽ ; burns △
Water	▽	downward	con- (-) cealing	dark	coarse	mobile	▽ extinguishes △ ; Saturates △ ▽ washes away △
Air	△	upward	self- (+) expressive	dark	fine	mobile	△ feeds △ ; absorbs ▽ ▽ moves △ & △
Earth	▽	downward	con- (-) cealing	dark	coarse	static	▽ needs, releases, and absorbs △ △

According to legend, the following pairs of elements are but two aspects of the same thing:

△ & △ are Father and Son, while

▽ & ▽ are Mother and Daughter.

composite of the Earth-Air-Water-Fire Elements. Their Earth in tissue and bone is made up of ninety-two-odd fundamental substances, which are the chemical elements that interlink in many different ways. Six of them (carbon, hydrogen, oxygen, nitrogen, phosphorous and sulfur) can do so to an almost unlimited extent. The carbon atom in particular has a fourfold ability to join itself to other atoms and thereby release energy. Without invisible air to breathe in and breathe out constantly, people could survive only for a very few minutes. Since two-thirds of a person's total weight consists of water, one would dehydrate without frequently replenishing what is constantly lost. Fire is hidden in the flameless metabolic combustion named oxidation-reduction-hydrolysis that occurs every second of life.

The Book of Daniel (2:31-33) describes the fourfold archetype of humankind vividly in Nebuchadnezzar's dream: "Thou, o King, sawest and beheld a great image. . . . This image's head was of fine gold, his breast and his arms of silver, his belly and his thighs of brass, his legs of iron, his feet in part of iron and part of clay."

The four-dimensional human body is deeply embedded in the Tree of Life. Illustrating humankind's true origin and ultimate reality of being, its spirit lives in the World of Origination, its soul dwells in the World of Creation, its heart and mind move in the World of Formation, and its physical body manifests in the World of Expression and Matter.

We can establish inner world contacts with the Four Worlds; by contemplation we reach the World of Origination, by meditation we contact the Creative World, by deep thinking and feeling we reach the World of Formation, and we *act* while in the World of Matter.

My Teacher illustrated the difference between meditation and contemplation by saying, "One is like love expressed in words, the other is the lover's embrace."

There is one more four-world analogy, truly sublime, to reflect upon and absorb. It is the sacrosanct four-letter name of the Lord God of the Hebrews: the Holy Tetragrammaton (meaning the word of four letters) YHVH, which is variously spelled IHVH or JHVH. The legitimate spelling is with the actual words of the four Hebraic letters, Yod He Vav He, and incorrectly rendered as Jehovah. The correct sound of the holy name is said to contain the immeasurable powers of the Four Elements of Life as they express the divine will. The pronunciation of the Tetragrammaton remains therefore concealed unless orally transmitted by one who knows its spelling to someone who is ready to receive it, and who, in turn, is committed to secrecy. Only the Rabbi may whisper the holy word on the Day of Atonement, alone with his God in the tabernacle of the Temple.

Now to the meaning of the four Hebrew letters. The letter Yod, a positive creative force and the foundation of the entire alphabet, is the well from which all letters flow. Its shape too, is a basic part of most of the twenty-two letters of the alphabet. In translation the letter Yod means the "open hand" that touches divine energy and light. The letter He signifies receptivity and the feminine principle of reproduction. It represents a transparent window, through which one may look out from the inside and in from the outside. The letter Vav is again a positive force that unites the

Yod with the first He. It means the "nail" which fastens and holds things together. The second He, the final letter, is again a receptive principle and a synthesis of the first three letters. It indicates where the reproductive offspring abides, while the first letter, He, signifies where its beginning has taken place.

The word YHVH as the holy name of the One God is truly fascinating in its grammar. It is a noun form derived from a verbal root which means "to be." Transliterated it stands for the being that is, was and is to be: *That* which ever was, *That* which is, *That* which shall ever be. In a very real sense, therefore, the letters Yod He Vav He signify—not merely a chosen name—but primarily a tangible, numerical word-principle or secret formula for the invisible and indivisible creative power.

In their physical form and essence the four Hebrew letters illustrate the figure of Adam Kadmon, the Creator's idea of a human as the individualized universe (Figure 16). The letter Yod is the head; the first letter He the arms and shoulders; the letter Vav the breast;

Figure 16. The Fourfold Body of Man
(The Prototypal "Adam Kadmon")

Yod	Head
He	Arms and Shoulders
Vav	Breast
He	Legs

and the second letter He the two legs. In this arrangement, each letter represents one of the Four Worlds.

True to the mysteries of the Tree of Life there is one unexpected twist. While it would seem appropriate that one letter would be residing in each one of the Tree's Four Worlds, it is not quite so. The letter Yod and the first letter He abide in the World of Creation, which signifies that the first two letters are creatively and eternally conjoined; the third letter Vav resides in the World of Formation; and the second letter He is in the World of Manifestation.

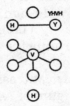

Why is there no letter abiding in the World of Origination? It is, as Meister Eckhart once said, that "God does not own." Thus the Godhead in his own World does not even "own" the first letter of his holy name, Yod.

It may be confusing to many that the entire Tetragrammaton YHVH has its abode in the second Tree branch in the World of Creation. This is because the "Wisdom of Creation" is the mirror of the Creator, the "I Am That I Am."

8
Trinity: Architect of Creation

In the Great Plan of Life, as in the Tree of Life, "the
Three are One" and "the One is in the Three." Called
the trinity, this ternary unity is variously referred to
as trigrammaton, and also as triangle or triad. Just as
Pythagoras saw the Number Three as the first geometrical shape with length, width and depth, so is a
trinity usually pictured as an equal-sided triangle.

The trinity reveals the underlying principle of balance expressed by the universal Laws of Life. Without balance, there would be chaos in the chain of
Life. Yet balance itself never is, and never should be,
permanent; it must be attained again and again
through reconciliation of conflicting currents. This
is why, on the earth plane, conflicts in the outside
world and conflicts within one's self are indispensable and actually constructive. My Teacher looked at
balance this way: "In all walks of life balance is
achieved when duality merges into oneness and
when otherness becomes sameness. There is no
peace and no harmony without balance; and there is

133

no progress without struggle. A paradox? Only apparently so. We need both balance and instability in equal measure."

The undivided oneness of the cosmic trinity is but the balanced union of two initial contraries by a uniting third. It illustrates a "self-existent unity" within three different states of existence and the ultimate harmony achieved through the "marriage of opposites." Perhaps the most apparent Law of Life in human existence, opposites may be regarded as constant sources of motion expressed in life. Their duality attracts, resists and separates, yet at the same time stimulates, complements and finally unites. Their tension and friction move toward creative manifestation. Thus, the trinity illustrates the mutual dissonance between opposites as they fuse into a union of complements, representing the unity behind all duality. In the universe the trinity provides the fundamental essence for creation to begin. On the human level it yields that pure harmony which leads to unfolding freedom.

The three-dimensional unity is at the core of every genuine tradition, including the ancient Chinese emblem of the Tao. There the masculine Yang and the feminine Yin unite within a circle to form the Diagram of the Supreme Ultimate. (Figure 17).

Cosmic triads are too numerous to count. They range from uppermost transcendental existence to terrestrial manifestation—from the Holy Trinity in all true religions to the humble three-leafed clover on nature's meadows. Touchable trinities of height, width and depth are everywhere, from the great blue whale to the tiny amoeba; from the peak of Mount Everest, five-and-a-half miles above sea level, to the

Figure 17. The Tao

Mariana Trench, seven miles deep in the Pacific Ocean. And yet most of us take trinities for granted, and only a very few are curious enough to ask for the real meaning of "the One that is Three" and "the Three that are One."

The Tree of Life offers important clues for comprehending the nature of the trinity. All its triads carry dynamic relationships among three equal powers whose presence together results in new harmony and progress. Its first power is always a positive, stimulating and creative masculine force; its second is always a negative, receptive and creating feminine form; and its third is always a "neutral" power that balances the existing duality. It cannot be otherwise.

This, briefly, is the story of the trinity. First attracted by opposition, and then linked in tension, energy is released providing the universally needed *friction* (another word for strife or struggle) which is basic to *growth*. This friction between two contending forces leads to a self-generating interrelationship. Its cosmic purpose is the essential *balance* (another word for stability or harmony) which is necessary for *progress*. Thereby, a new bond is established in which "the three are as one" and "the one is the three" at the same time.

You will find many representations and typical

examples in this book. Ponder them. A clearer understanding of the trinity's eminent significance will
make a lasting imprint on the quality of your everyday thoughts and actions.

The Tree of Life separates naturally into two distinct triple trinity patterns, with each offering an
altogether different insight into the multi-aspected
ternary essence of life. The first and horizontal triple
trinity of creation (Figure 18) forms three triangles by

Figure 18. The Triple Trinity of Creation

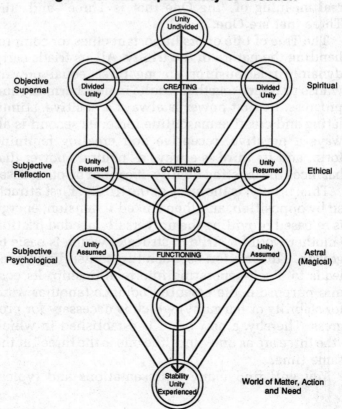

grouping the Tree branches One, Two and Three; Four, Five and Six; and Seven, Eight and Nine. It illustrates the three-step evolution of universal life. The second and vertical triple trinity pattern—the Three Pillars in the Tree of Life (Figure 20)—groups the ten Tree branches into three upright columns; it pictures the blueprint of balanced harmony, and—again—of freedom.

I. The Triple-Trinity of Creation

Of the three horizontal triangles in the Tree of Life (Figure 18), each has its own specific function. The upper Supernal or Celestial Triangle represents the Trinity of Existence. This triad is objective because it embraces the two Worlds of Origination and Creation. As the self-existent container of divine consciousness, it expresses the root powers and dynamic essence of creation: the Spiritual World. Stimulated by the two contrasting archetypal powers at work— the creative force of Wisdom and the creating form of Understanding—"Unity Divided" is balanced by an upward pointing beam in "Unity Undivided," the oneness of the Creator. And creation is thus ready to move ahead.

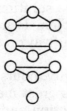

The nature of the middle and lower triangles is subjective because they dwell in the World of Formation; their uniting beams point downward, and thus these two triads must find their own balance. The middle *Ethical Triangle* or Triangle of Virtue is the reflection or mirror image of the upper. It depicts the "unity resumed" with the governing principles that establish the universe: the moral world. The base Astral or Magical (sometimes named astro-physical) Triangle is the lower arc of the middle trinity. It presents the "unity assumed" with the functioning forces of polarity working toward later expression in unity. Contrary to the first triad, these two trinities must attain and maintain their own stability for the benefit of the tenth Tree branch: the World of Matter, our planet Earth.

All three triangles have this in common: (1) They are cosmically "protected" by one veil, heralding a change in vibration. One veil separates the Supernal from the Ethical Triangle and indicates the change from illuminated awareness to cosmic consciousness. The veil of Paroketh separates the ethical from the astro-physical triad, and marks the descent of nonmaterial force into material form; and it heralds the ascent of what is terrestrial to that which is divine. (2) The contrasting powers of each trinity always emanate from the Tree branches on the horizontal line and meet in their uniting beam (the third Tree branch) exactly at the midway point. This transcendental fact applies also to terrestrial matters. This is to say that the solution of any practical human dispute or problem is never found on either side. It lies always midway on a third and harmonizing beam.

The threefold trinity pours all cosmic essences continuously into its great magnet and sole recipient—the World of Action and Need. There unity is experienced by: (1) the creative root powers of the Supernal Triangle where force and form oppose and complement each other; (2) the governing forces of the Ethical Triangle where overabundance and restriction find balance in morality; and (3) the functioning forces from the Astral Triangle where passion and reason struggle to find harmony.

While each trinity shows how "three are one," its deepest meaning becomes crystal clear by looking at the qualities of its respective Tree branches.

There the Supernal Triangle demonstrates the "eternal marriage in heaven." Its first power (the Crown) is the ever-becoming Godhead; its second power (Wisdom) is the limitless active force without form, the eternal male; and its third power (Understanding) the receiving and limiting, yet life-producing and reproducing passive form, the eternal female. The two forces of creation find their balance in the godhead without the latter's actual manifestation. And in so doing creation reveals its reason and purpose for existence: the Creator's will, desire and need to manifest as tangible matter. Its purpose is division (separation) for the sake of reunion. Or we might say, it is Light longing to become Life, and Force yearning to have Form.

The *Ethical Triangle* shows activity. There we experience the fundamental principles of universal government in the ideal marriage of an unselfish and generous Lord of Heaven with an equally unselfish Lord of Justice. Yet before their union can occur in the heart of the Tree, all necessary restrictions in defense of law and order must be put to work, and all the waste piled up by indiscriminate generosity must go. To find harmony betwixt and between overabundance and restriction demands the very highest level of morality and integrity of purpose, of design and character. In everyday terms, think of a child as the apex of a family triangle in which restriction and abundance must be imparted in equal portions by the parents to provide the basic foundation of morality. "Ethical" is therefore the appropriate name for this triad; and the word also indicates life's reason and purpose.

The *Astral or Magical Triangle* illustrates the functioning forces of polarity in their perpetual endeavor to reach stability. It presents the mystical marriage of Anima, the intuitive Lady of Love, with Animus, the pragmatic Lord of Books and Learning. Yet before the two are able to unite in the multifaceted machinery of the universe, the strong forces of unbridled feelings must come to harmonious terms with the potent forms of discriminative thought. This is no easy task, and the relentless struggle for utmost clarity is imperative. Balance must be maintained between all magical, psychic, astral and etheric powers, including the ever-changing moon and the easily deceiving Treasure House of Images. And because this triad's balancing beam lies in what is rightly called the "visible drapery around an invisible framework," this last triangle fulfills its reason and purpose by piercing through this invisible framework in order to be visible behind gross matter-to-be.

The triple trinity of universal life expresses itself in the color relationships of the Tree branches as the reflected colors of nature—the Creative World. It comes as no surprise that the colors appear in the first triad with the neutrals: white, gray (a mixture of white and black) and black; in the second triad with the primary colors: red, yellow, and blue; and in the third triad with the secondary colors as mixtures of primary colors (Figure 19).

Figure 19. The Trinities in Color

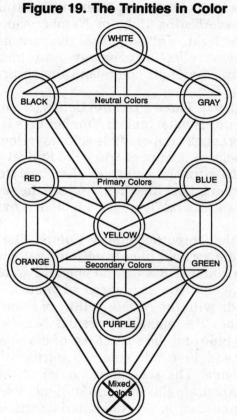

Kabbalists refer to the color sequences on the branches of the Tree of Life as "mezla," which in Hebrew means the "hidden influence" from light to darkness. And it is this hidden influence that carries the color of each Tree branch. Here's how.

First, the Three *Neutrals*. Tree branch Number One is white brilliance; branch Number Two as a mirror image of Number One is iridescent gray; and the receptive branch Number Three is black. The contrasting colors of Tree branches Two and Three illustrate their extreme polarity and their eternal link to the brilliant, everlasting light of Number One. When seen in the light, white signifies the presence of all colors and the reflection of energy, while black signifies the absence of all colors and the absorption of energy.

Second, the Three *Primary Colors*. Tree branch Number Four is blue; branch Number Five is scarlet-red; and branch Number Six is golden-yellow. As the mirror image of the upper triad, the Ethical Triangle reflects the primary colors of the Creative World which, when mixed together, produce the secondary colors of the Astral Triangle. Light is moving into Life.

Third, the Three *Secondary Colors*. The blue of branch Number Four blends with the golden-yellow of branch Number Six for the emerald green in the Number Seven; the scarlet-red of branch Number Five blends with the golden-yellow of branch Number Six into the orange of branch Number Eight; while the blue and the scarlet-red of branches Number Four and Five mix into the purple of branch Number Nine. The secondary colors of the Astral Triangle illustrate the increase in density from fine spirit to gross matter, as non-material force begins to take shape as material form.

In summary, the Tree of Life's three horizontal triangles illustrate and clarify humankind's great legacy and undeniable heritage: universal freedom. Cradled in the plan of creation and firmly ingrained in our inner spaces, freedom is the inborn ability to *choose to be your real self*. To do so, conflicts of thoughts, feelings and actions must be resolved by defining your reason for existence and your purpose in life. In the final analysis, such freedom is an unshakable self-confidence without fear. It is the inward trust that everything has an essential—even irreplaceable—part in the one reality of life. The triple trinity of creation provides some answers as to what lies within as well as without, in the macrocosm and in the microcosm. It is to feel, think, intuit, create and procreate, while seeing, hearing, smelling, tasting, touching and loving the reality of freedom.

II. *The Three Pillars: Blueprint of Harmony*

The vertical division of the Tree of Life displays its branches in three parallel columns called Pillars (Figure 20). This perspective presents an altogether different picture of the universe and you. It is a cosmic blueprint of balance between creative and receptive polarities. Expressed in terrestrial terms, the three Pillars tell of the human soul's journey to freedom on the middle path of harmony between the powers of force and form.

Each of the two outside pillars has within it three Tree branches; the center column contains four branches. The name of Mercy for the column at the right and of Severity for the column at the left is derived from the Tree branch in the center of each respective triad. The fourfold center Pillar (sometimes referred to as the Perfect Pillar) is called Mildness. It illustrates states of cosmic awareness.

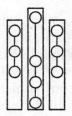

Figure 20. The Three Pillars of Manifest Existence

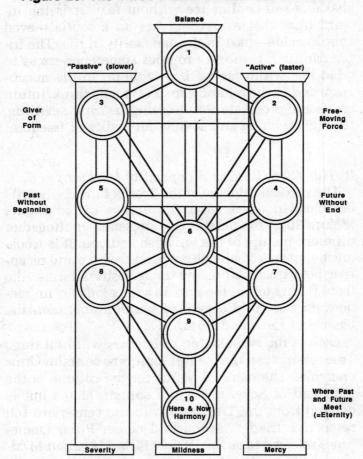

The two outer Pillars of Mercy and Severity pinpoint their overall functions in life's primary polarities. Both have less freedom than the balancing center Pillar of Mildness. It is not by coincidence that the harmonizing neutral center beams of the Tree's horizontal triangles find their home in the balancing Pillar of Mildness.

Probing the qualities of the three Pillars in greater detail, we find that the nondiscriminating right pillar of Mercy and Compassion symbolizes the creative, active, positive or electric transmitter of life—the initiating male principle. Without engaging in specific directions, it projects its fast-moving, formless force of orally transmitted wisdom into the eternal tomorrow, a future without end. The discriminating left Pillar of Severity and Austerity represents the receptive and transforming giver of form, the passive, negative or magnetic creating female principle. It gives a direction and illustrates the slow-moving, preserving form transmitted by the written word, a wisdom which comes from an ever-present past that has no beginning. The center Pillar of Mildness and Serenity symbolizes the eternal here and now and expresses harmony, balance and the reality of freedom.

It is no accident, but rather scripted within life's great plan, that the center Pillar of Mildness holds four (and not three) Tree branches in its column. It illustrates thereby one of the Tree's great messages, which is expressed as a fourfold action: the Crown (1) has found its King (6); together they have laid the Foundation (9), and have established the Kingdom (10) on Earth. In other words, the one radiant light from above has become radiating love, and love has become life. Infinite life force has become finite matter and the invisible Unmanifest has become visibly manifest as humankind and nature.

The Pillar of Mildness also defines the four levels of ascending human consciousness. In the Kingdom (10) human beings have both sense perception and earth awareness. In the Foundation (9) they acquire a psychic and somehow automatic consciousness. In Beauty the King (6) they gain cosmic consciousness, and in the Crown (1) attain illumination.

According to legend, the Tree of Life's two outer Pillars stood tall in the Temple of Solomon. There the patriarch Abraham symbolized Mercy, and his son Isaac represented Severity. Between the two stood the human archetype, in the center Pillar of Mildness. In the light of truth and freedom it sought for their guidance, and partook of their power.

By analogy the right Pillar parallels the Yang of the Tao, and the left Pillar the Yin. In Kabbalistic astrology we shall encounter the three *gunas* (modes of action) of the Hindus: the active *rajas* quality (synonymous with the Pillar of Mercy); the reactive and receptive *tamas* (in step with the Pillar of Severity); and the balanced *sattwa* (conforming with the Pillar of Mildness). Another identity is to be found in the Major Arcana of the Tarot deck. Therein the High Priestess (card number two) sits between Jachin in the white Pillar (of Mercy) at her left, and Boaz in the black Pillar (of Severity) at her right (I Kings 7:21).

If we place the three upright trinities over the perpetually emanating Lightning Flash of Life, its descending path is seen to touch the Tree branches from One to Ten, one by one, and thus tie the three Pillars to the path of creation.

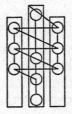

First it binds the harmony of Mildness to the force of Mercy, then to the form of Severity, and by repeating this pattern successively, it travels in zigzag fashion from the top to the bottom of the center Pillar of Mildness. In so doing, the miraculous web of interacting, ever-changing and often contradictory power vibrations called the Laws of Life express the modes of harmony and balance. In the endless chain of life these expressions are themselves the effect which keeps on becoming a new beginning.

It may come as a surprise that the author of the Tree of Life pictogram secretly built the mystical Tree of Knowledge into an inspiring symbol. By exchanging the paradisal metaphor of good and evil with the symbolic Pillars of Mercy and Severity, and with the three pairs of opposites in the Tree of Life, another practical dimension has been added to our understanding of ourselves and the universe. It is the Trinity of Freedom, formed by our free will, the duality of manifest existence and the harmony achieved through the integration by making opposites complements.

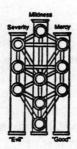

After eating of the forbidden fruit, Adam and Eve fell from their blissful primordial "oneness" into the duality of the world of opposites. As the Bible allegory tells us, it is the familiar story of the Fall. In their

nakedness they became aware of each other's "otherness" and its consequences. Ever since that decisive
moment in the Garden of Eden, humankind has been
compelled incessantly to differentiate and choose
between this and that, between good and evil, right
and wrong, male and female, night and day, yes and
no, and all the rest of it. And in so doing, the price for
exercising free will is constantly paid and repaid.

Good and evil are the opposite poles of one reality
and, as such, they are neither good nor evil. A ther-
mometef, for instance, cannot tell where hot ends
and cold begins; for both are the same thing, namely
temperature which manifests as either hot or cold
according to a judgment resulting from free choice.
Take food for example. If your body consumes more
food than it needs, an increase in weight results. But
the same food, properly balanced according to personal needs, will keep your physical body in good
form. Food is neither good nor evil; yet the human
body can be a garbage collector or a temple of God.
Again, within free will each must decide.

As long as we are on planet Earth and live in duality, it is only human that we think in terms of right
and wrong, of good and evil. This is an ethical problem conditioned by individuals' awareness of the
needs of their community. The ancient mysteries of
Egypt and Greece give some clues to this problem.
*Evil is any deed or expressed thought which causes
suffering to any living thing including oneself.* Self-
ishness is another evil because it disrupts the harmony of one's environment.

The concept of good and evil is not infallible, for it
is subjective. Where does the good end and the evil
begin? You may call a thing "evil" which I consider
"good." Conversely, what may be "good" for you,
may be "evil" for another human being. The follow-

ing are two well-known quotations (from the Bible and Shakespeare) regarding good and evil, and a few unsolicited opinions gathered during the last years from students of the Tree of Life:

Job 2:10: "Shall we receive good at the hand of God, and shall we not receive evil?"

Hamlet: "There is neither good or bad, but thinking makes it so."

"Evil is thoughts and deeds in opposition to the Laws of Life."

"It's simple. With religion being the science of good and evil, I *know* what's good or evil."

"Good and evil are within maya; they are therefore unreal."

"Good and evil are not things but conditions."

"Good is seen by means of evil."

"There is only good, but man's lack of balance produces evil."

"Nothing is either good or evil. But our experience will be good or evil depending on how we understand its relativity."

Before the never-ending story of the universal trinities comes to a temporary halt—with repeated references to be made in future chapters—let us digress for a moment, and reflect on the eleven triangu-

Figure 21. Trinities From the Heart of the Tree of Life

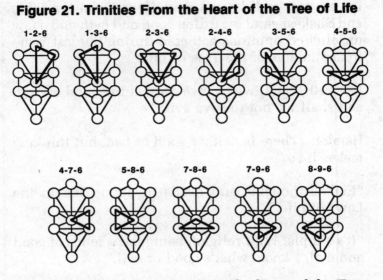

lar relationships emerging from the heart of the Tree of Life, its branch Number Six named Beauty the King. The numbers of the branch triads are added to the diagrams (Figure 21) as a practical aid in your meditations on the heartbeat of the Tree.

9

IN THE COMPANY OF ANGELS

More numerous than human beings, their number is legion, their names are many, their ranks and tasks are varied and widespread in a network of celestial hierarchies. (*Hieros* means sacred and *archo* to govern.) Known as angels, these selfless intermediaries between God and humankind have an important part in religious life, especially in the Zoroastrian, Judeo-Christian and Muhammadan traditions.

Angels have more than symbolic and poetic significance in thought and scripture. As fellow workers of the Creator, they are messengers of divinity, not winged people with haloes, nor departed souls that flutter around in luminous robes. They have no physical bodies, carry no weight of the flesh; their "bodies" are far finer than ours, and can travel to faraway places in an instant. Sometimes they appear to man as human beings. Angels have no gender, no age, no wants, no desires, and usually no word-expression except for the glories they sing in unison. They have no will of their own, make no decisions except to do the will of the Creator, follow divine commands faithfully, and leave no task unfinished.

Angels are transcendental beings and vehicles for divine action. They are Powers of Light and instruments to assist the Creator in governing the universe. Their life force never fades; they are immortal but not eternal, as nothing but God is eternal. As fellow workers they carry God's messages to humanity, serve as divine guardians for humankind and provide the ladder for our ascent to divinity.

Since the beginning of time, angels have always been near God. They were present when the world was created and were the first "select heavenly company" in paradise. They studied his eternal wisdom, and in turn, remained his constant "divine council."

Thirty-five of the Bible's sixty-six books, including those of early biblical times, tell of angels in the same manner as the ancient Hindu scriptures mention their *devas*. It is not surprising, therefore, that the angelic hierarchies of two major religions (the Jewish and the Christian) are based on the Tree of Life. The Hebrew tradition follows its four-world pattern; the pseudo-Dionysian Christian tradition conforms with its trinity division. The qualities of both the Tree branches and all angelic hierarchies magnify one another.

I. Angels In the Four Worlds

The Hebrew tradition has two ways of presenting angels in the Four Worlds. In the first and single-Tree grouping, each of the ten Tree branches has—in addition to its divine name — a ruling archangel, an angelic order and a residing planet. (Chapter 7 and Figure 22.)

Figure 22. Angels in the Four Worlds
(In Space Version One)

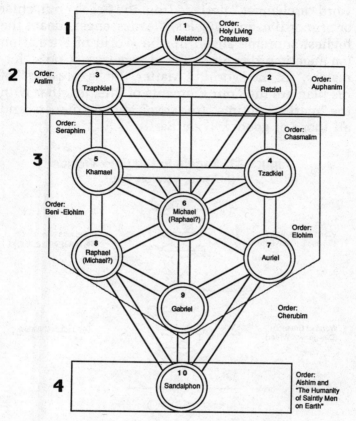

The second classification places a full Tree of Life in each of the Four Worlds (Figure 23). But whatever four-world system is used, the Godhead acts directly only in the first world; and does so by emanating his great plan with the sounds of his self-given divine names. In each of the successively emerging three worlds, God's word directs his angels to execute and manifest his will. Thus, in the Creative World, his ordained "creators" are the ten archangels. (The word "archangel," derived from the Greek *arch*, chief or primordial, and *angelos*, the messenger, means the highest supreme angel.) In the World of Formation ten angelic orders or choirs of angels are God's "formators." In the World of Matter, the "expressors" of his plan are the Four Elements of Life, together with the "markers of time" (the seven ancient planets) and all those of good will on Earth.

Figure 23. Angels in the Four Worlds
(In Time, Version Two)

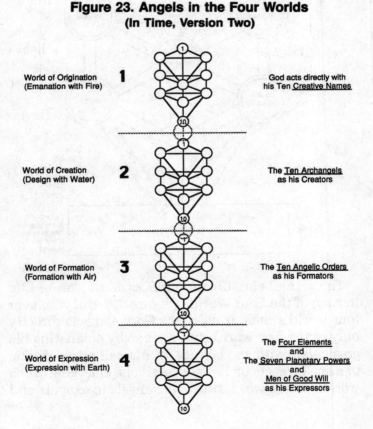

World of Origination
(Emanation with Fire)   **1**   God acts directly with
his Ten <u>Creative Names</u>

World of Creation
(Design with Water)   **2**   The <u>Ten Archangels</u>
as his Creators

World of Formation
(Formation with Air)   **3**   The <u>Ten Angelic Orders</u>
as his Formators

World of Expression
(Expression with Earth)   **4**   The <u>Four Elements</u>
and
The <u>Seven Planetary Powers</u>
and
<u>Men of Good Will</u>
as his Expressors

The names of the archangels indicate how close they are to the Creator. For all except the first and tenth names end with the letters *El*, meaning "the Lord."

Metatron is archangel to the Crown and to the divine name of Eheieh. The name resembles Meta Ton Thronon, and means the Great Teacher, and Beside the Throne. But he has other titles. Angel of Presence (Isaiah 63:9), Prince of Faces, Center within the Circle, and Chancellor of Heaven are among them. As Angel of Elohim he oversees all creation. He alone sees God face to face, and is the king and chief of all ministering angels.

According to legend, Metatron is the youngest archangel and also the tallest angel in the heavens. At one time he was "Enoch who was not, for God took him" (Genesis 5:24). As the guardian and ruler of the prophet Moses, he led the Hebrews through their forty years in the Sinai. The Talmud tells that to this day Metatron also teaches prematurely dead children in paradise.

The *Angelic Order* corresponding to the Crown [and also to the Christian Seraphim*] is the Chaioth ha Qadesh or Holy Living Creatures. In Ezekiel's vision they are the animals "like burning coals of fire" and "going round about the Throne," as mentioned in Revelation. The parallel power in the planetary sphere is the prime mover, the Primum Mobile.

Ratziel is archangel to Wisdom and to the Divine name of Jehovah. He is the Herald of Deity, entrusted with guarding and transmitting divine secrets. As-

---

*All Christian attributions refer to the Angelic Hierarchy of Dionysius the Areopagite, and are put in [ ] brackets.

cribed to this archangel is the *Book of the Angel Ratziel*. It is said that the book's secrets were told to Adam when he was driven from paradise; later they were revealed to Noah as he entered the ark before the deluge, and were ultimately conveyed to Solomon the Wise.

Furthermore, legend tells that Ratziel still proclaims the secrets of his book to all humankind from the top of Mount Horeb every day.

Corresponding to Wisdom [and also to the Christian cherubim] the *Angelic Order of Auphanim* keeps the Wheel of creation turning, a hint at the zodiac wheel residing in the sephirah Wisdom.

Tzaphkiel is archangel to Understanding and to the divine name of Jehovah Elohim. He is the Beholder of God, and frequently called the Contemplation of God. His parallel planetary sphere is Saturn.

The *Angelic Order of Aralim*, corresponding to Understanding [and also to the Christian Thrones], is called the Mighty Ones on the Thrones of Mysteries.

Tzadkiel, archangel to Mercy and to the divine name of El, is the Righteous of God, sometimes titled the Justice of God, Angel of Divine Justice and the Holy One. He was the angel protecting Abraham the Patriarch, and is also the angel of the planet Jupiter abiding in the same sphere.

The *Angelic Order of Chasmalim*, corresponding to Mercy [and also the Christian Dominions], is called the Brilliant or Shining Ones, and the Scintillating Flames.

Khamael, archangel to Severity-Justice and to the divine name of Elohim Gebor, is the Severity of God, the Right Hand of God, and, in personifying divine justice, the Burner of God. In Druid mythology his name is the God of War.

The *Angelic Order of Seraphim*, corresponding to Severity-Justice [and also to the Christian Holy Virtues], is the Powers of the Fiery or Flaming Serpents. The Hebrew word *seraphim* means serpent. According to myth, the prophet Moses, at one time during his stay in the wilderness, raised a Seraphim of Brass. Here, the parallel planetary power sphere is Mars.

Michael, archangel corresponding to Beauty the King and to the divine name of Aloah va Daath, is the Perfect of God, Who is Like unto God, and the Destroyer of Evil. He and the archangel Raphael are the two chief Ruling Princes in the entire angelic hierarchy. So much so that some Kabbalists like to assign Raphael's residence to this, and not to the eighth Tree branch.

In apocryphal literature, Michael is described as the celestial high priest and protector of Israel. He is a healer, the keeper of the keys to heaven and Satan's main adversary. He came to Mary in order to announce her approaching death. In biblical and post-biblical lore and also in Jewish, Christian, Islamic and Persian writings, Michael ranks amongst the greatest of archangels. When Michael wept, his tears formed precious stones, so legend tells.

The *Angelic Order of Malachim*, Messengers or Kings, corresponding to Beauty the King [and also to the Christian Powers], is called the Balancers. Their parallel planetary power sphere is the Sun.

Auriel (*Uriel* or *Haniel*), archangel to Victory-Firmness and to the divine name of Jehovah Tzabaoth, is the Grace of God, the Light of God and also the Face of God. In noncanonical lore, he watches over thunder and terror as the angelic Fire of God. He was the messenger sent by God to Noah to herald the approaching deluge (Enoch I, 10:1-3). Auriel wrestled with Jacob and then changed his name to Israel. He visited Ezra to tell him about the great mysteries of the universe. Among his many duties, he was to lead the later Patriarch Abraham out of Ur.

The *Angelic Order of the Elohim*, corresponding to Victory [and also to the Christian Principalities], is called the Divine, at times also the Brilliant Ones and the Guardians of Nature. Here the parallel planetary power sphere is Venus.

Raphael, archangel corresponding to Glory in Splendor and to the divine name of Elohim Tzabaoth, is the Heavenly Physician, the Teacher of Mankind, the Angel of the Four Winds, the Angel of the Presence, and the Healer of Wounds. Together with the archangels Gabriel, Michael and Auriel, Raphael is guarding the four points of the camp of Israel and the four corners of the world. He is especially revered as angel of healing by treating all illnesses and injuries. It is believed that he defends humankind from the attacks of demons. Reaching further, he protects and guides travelers. As already mentioned, some Kabbalists think that Michael (from Beauty the King) belongs to this Tree branch as the mighty warrior fighting the war in heaven (Revelation 12:7-8).

The *Angelic Order of the Beni Elohim*, corresponding to Glory [and also to the Christian Archangels], is composed of the Sons of God who, as written in Genesis, took the daughters of men for wives. Their parallel planetary power sphere is Mercury.

Gabriel, archangel to the Foundation and to the name of Shaddai El Chai, is called God is My Strength and the Man-God of Life. His missions are diversified. As the Potent of God, he presides over paradise. He is the Divine Messenger carrying divine decrees. Bearing a trumpet (which originally was a horn of fertility), he is the Angel of Annunciation, informing the Virgin Mary of the blessed event. He also announced the birth of John the Baptist to his father Zacharias (Luke 1:11-20). It is said that he carried Abraham on his back to Babylon. According to Jewish lore, he dealt with the sinful cities of Sodom and Gomorrah. In Islamic tradition, Gabriel dictated the entire Koran to Muhammad, the prophet of Allah.

The *Angelic Order of the Cherubim*, corresponding to the Foundation [and also to the Christian Angels], is the Seat of Sons known as the Strong Watchers. Sometimes the *Angelic Order of Aishim*, meaning Souls of Fire, is also designated for this Tree branch. According to Genesis 3:24, winged Cherubim stand watch in the East of the garden of Eden "to keep the way of the Tree of Life." And furthermore, two pure golden cherubim were placed over the Ark of the Covenant in the Tabernacle of Solomon's Temple to guard the ark and conceal its emanating power and glory (Exodus 25:10-22 and I Kings 8:6-8). In Ezekiel's famous vision (Ezekiel 10:14), the winged cherubim are the four-faced bearers of the Divine Throne, [cherub, man, lion and eagle] — a reminder of the winged sphinx in Egyptian mythology. Their parallel planetary power sphere is Levanah, the moon.

Sandalphon is archangel to the two God names of Adonai Malekh (meaning the Lord and King) and Adonai ha Aretz (meaning the Lord made Manifest in Nature) in the Kingdom. Said to be the twin brother of Metraton, Sandalphon is the Mediator, and sometimes named the Messiah. His Greek name lends itself to several hazy interpretations; it *may* mean Lord of the Height, Co-Brother, or Sound of Sandals. His abode is in the Four Elements of Life and in the sphere of the Seven Planetary Powers.

The *Angelic Order of Aishim*, corresponding to the Kingdom, has a reflective and protective fire. Named the Souls of Fire, this order is assisted in its work by the Humanity of Saintly Men of Earth [the Christian Lovers of God].

It is worthy of note that four archangels of old are still very popular in the Western world and adorn many altars and portals in Christian churches. They direct the Four Elements of Life in the four corners of the universe in addition to their numerous celestial missions.

Raphael, whose eminent quality is charity, stands in the east and balances Air. *Michael*, whose exalted quality is holiness, stands in the south and controls Fire. *Gabriel*, whose prominent quality is strength, stands in the west and directs Water. And *Auriel*, whose towering quality is knowledge, stands in the north. He watches over Nature's fertility and fights against the further pollution of our so badly contaminated soil.

II. *Angels in the Trinities*
The Dionysian "Angels" follow the horizontal triple trinity pattern in the Tree of Life, as already men-

tioned (Figure 24). This celestial hierarchy of the sixth-century Christian mystic Dionysius the Areopagite has occupied an essential part in Christian theology and liturgy to this day.[12] Following passages in the Old and New Testaments,[13] it consists of nine celestial choirs (sometimes named Intelligences), and includes a tenth choir as the Hierarchs on Earth. The latter are called "Lovers of God" because their lives express divinity. A representative listing of these fellow workers of God would include

Figure 24. Angels in Trinities
(Dionysian)

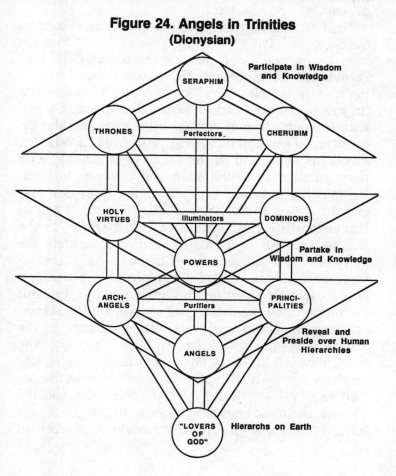

the Old Testament's hierarch Melchizedek, and probably Daniel and Joseph whose visions came through angels. In modern times, the listing may possibly name several Christian saints, the humanitarian Albert Schweitzer and Mother Teresa of Calcutta.

The names of the nine orders in this celestial hierarchy signify their divine attributes and godlike qualities. Each triad is directed by the one above, and all are inspired by the highest intelligence, the seraphim. The last order, named simply angels, is in closest contact with humanity.

The first angelic trinity, called the Lords, dwells in the Supernal Triangle of the Tree of Life. They are "the perfectors" and participate in wisdom and knowledge. In the Crown are the six-winged "glowing" Seraphim (Numbers 21:6 and Isaiah 6:2,6) as the fiery serpents and Lords of Love. They are concerned with the evolution of eternal principles and the inspiration of humankind with divine love. In Wisdom dwell the cherubim as the Lords of Harmony, who pray, participate in the stream of wisdom, and enlighten the minds of humans. They intercede and guard the way to the Tree of Life (Genesis 3:24). In Understanding, the Thrones of Steadfastness, as the Divine Seats of the Lords of Will, contemplate the glory of divine judgment. All three celestial perfectors participate in God's infinite power and wisdom, and, as already mentioned, their task is to transmit the orders they receive to the second trinity below.

The second and middle trinity conforms to the Ethical Triangle in the Tree of Life. They are "the illuminators." In Mercy are the eminently loving Dominions who radiate authority and regulate the activities of all angels. In Severity abide the godlike Virtues, the most energetic order with the gift of performing miracles: the Spirits of Movement. And in

Beauty the King dwell the order of Powers or Divine Reception.

The third and base trinity conforms with the Astral Triangle. In it are the Purifiers, sometimes called the Sons. In Victory they are the Principalities or Princes of Princes. In Glory the purifiers are the Archangels who, as the Sons of Fire, announce and reveal; furthermore they preside over all human hierarchies and direct the evolution of nations. And in Foundation they are the Angels who, as the Sons of Light, guide people on earth, and together with the archangels convey important messages when needed.

The nine Celestial Orders of Dionysius are mentioned in the *Theogony* of Hesiod. There the Greek poet tells us that a brazen anvil would take nine days to fall to Earth from Mount Olympus. This little story seems to illustrate that, at one time, all humankind will have to pass through these nine celestial orders.

Said Hazrat I. Khan: "The angels are not as great as man because—though they are gifted with the higher knowledge and dwell in the higher spheres—they have in general no power of expression; whereas man receives his knowledge from the higher source and expresses it through the means provided by the lower spheres."

The question is often asked: Are we able to contact the angels? The answer is a qualified yes. When a sincere human mind in cosmic consciousness reaches the angelic vibrations in harmony and silence, then the divine mind can impress the human consciousness. According to Kabbalistic tradition, we can reach all archangels from Metatron down to Sandalphon by way of the soul, that is through meditation. We can reach all angelic orders from the Holy Living Creatures down to the cherubim by way of the mind, that is through prayer. Since both meditation and prayer abide in the heart, we can reach the angels by way of our heart.

Of course it may take time to unlock your door to the world of angels. But sooner or later, humankind will learn and earn it, as did all saintly men and women in the past and those alive today.

*Initial Hebrew Letters of
the Ten Sephiroth*

10
Ten Plus Twenty-Two = Thirty-Two Highways to Wisdom

In Kabbalistic tradition, the Lord God formed the universe with his three powers of expression: Numbers, the Sound of the spoken word, and the written Word. So far, we have looked at the ten branches of the Tree of Life primarily as Numbers.

The twenty-two paths that connect the Tree branches represent primarily the twenty-two letters of the Hebrew alphabet. Created, made and formed by the Lord God as his tools for the sounds of creation, each letter represents one aspect of universal life. By being numerical as well as symbolical, the twenty-two letters are far more than mere vehicles for the sound of words. For the Lord God designed and formed these letters as his means to create and produce the Elements, the planets, the zodiacal signs, and all the corresponding bodily organs in humans. "He formed by means of them the whole creation and everything yet to be created," so tells *The Book of Formation* (Chapter II:2).

And yet the opening words of *The Book of Formation* tie the Tree's branches and paths together as the one foundation of all things: "In thirty-two mysterious paths of wisdom did the Lord God create his universe . . . with ten ineffable sephiroth . . . and twenty-two basal letters."[14] In this context, Tree branches and paths dovetail like complementary colors, and are never "instead of" but always "in addition to" one another. Their holistic oneness of substance and form may be considered the geometric design of the reality of existence.

Before we embark on the story of the Twenty-two Paths of Wisdom, further exploration into the mystery, tradition and message of the Hebrew alphabet is needed.

THE HEBREW ALPHABET

According to *The Book of Formation*, the Hebrew Alphabet (Figure 25) was written and formed by the living God. From the One Spirit "whose beginning has no beginning and whose end has no ending" came Air. And he formed therein twenty-two basal sounds; they are the letters and "the Spirit is first and above them." "From the Air, he formed Water, and from Water, he formed Fire."

It is an all-consonant alphabet because—in keeping with Jewish folklore—consonants are "the body of the word of God." Since vowels are considered "the soul of the word of God," they can have no physical presence in this sacred alphabet. It was not until the twelfth century A.D. that the interpolation of "vowel dots" was permitted to ease the pronunciation of words. The alphabet's square glyphs are often referred to as a "flame" alphabet because all of

Figure 25. The Hebrew Alphabet
R = regular letter   L = final letter

the letters have their primal foundation in the flame shape the tenth and central cipher Yod.

In addition to their individual essence, all letters share three qualities: number value by being primarily a number: sound by being the initial of a name; and word value (idea) by being pronounced as a full word. From 1 to 1000 (Table 4), the twenty-two letters allow a threefold division. The numbers from 1 to 10 represent the archetypes of numbers; those from 20 to 100 describe the archetypes in their cosmic states; and the numbers from 200 to 1000 illustrate the archetypes in their exalted states.

Table 4

THE HEBREW ALPHABET
In Numerical Order from One to Twenty-Two

Letter Form	Sequence	Number Value	Power	English (*)	Meaning	The Final Letters
	1	One	Mother	Aleph	Ox or Bull	
	2	Two	Double	Beth	House	**The Final Letters**
	3	Three	Double	Gimel	Camel	
	4	Four	Double	Daleth	Door	Kaph 500
	5	Five	Simple	He	Window	
	6	Six	Simple	Vav	Nail	Mem 600
	7	Seven	Simple	Zayin	Sword	
	8	Eight	Simple	Cheth	Fence	
	9	Nine	Simple	Teth	Serpent	Nun 700
	10	Ten	Simple	Yod	Hand	
	11	Twenty	Double	Kaph	Palm of Hand	Pe 800
	12	Thirty	Simple	Lamed	Oxgoad	
	13	Forty	Mother	Mem	Water	
	14	Fifty	Simple	Nun	Fish	Sadi 900
	15	Sixty	Simple	Samekh	Prop	
	16	Seventy	Simple	Ayin	Eye	1000
	17	Eighty	Double	Pe	Mouth	
	18	Ninety	Simple	Sadi	Fish Hook	
	19	Hundred	Simple	Koph	Back of Head	(*)
	20	Two hundred	Double	Resh	Head	The Random House Dictionary, 1966
	21	Three hundred	Mother	Shin	Tooth	
	22	Four hundred	Double	Tav	Tau Cross	

Numbers 1 to 10 — the archetypes.
Numbers 20 to 100 describe the process of the archetypes in their cosmic states.
Numbers 200 to 1000 express the exalted archetypes in their cosmic states.

In Table 4 each letter is followed by two numbers. The numeral next to the Hebrew letter-form indicates its sequential order in the alphabet from number 1 to 22. The other number marks its numerical Hebrew value which is greater than its sequential value after the tenth letter.

The Creator himself divided the alphabet threefold into: three mother letters, seven double letters and twelve simple letters (Figure 26). We shall meet the triad, the heptad and the dodecad again in the chapter on astrology.

Figure 26. The Hebrew Alphabet Illustrated

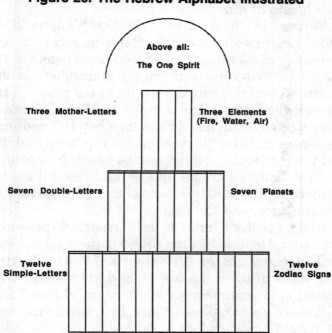

The *three mother letters* (Aleph, Mem and Shin) are the alphabet's interacting and interdependent exalted qualities. They are often simply referred to as "the Mothers." Because of a precious secret within them, they are sealed with six seals in the six directions of sacred space (Figure 28). From the Mothers proceed the three elements, balanced in oneness: Fire above, Water below and Air to balance the two. "Fathers were produced by them [the progenitors, meaning the first ones] and from the fathers descended the generations." From the letter Aleph comes air and the moistness; from Mem wet water and cold; and from Shin dry fire and heat. Mem is silent like water. Shin hisses like fire. Aleph is mediating between the other two like the invisible, almost voiceless breath of air.

We read in *The Book of Formation* (Chapter III, 8-10): "He caused the letter Aleph to reign in Air, bound a crown upon it and fused them together. He produced by means of them: the atmosphere in the universe, and the temperate state in the year. . . . He caused the letter Mem to reign in Water, bound a crown upon it and fused them together. He produced by means of them the earth of the universe, and the cold in the year. . . . He caused the letter Shin to reign in Fire, bound a crown upon it and fused them together. He produced by means of them the heavens in the universe, and the heat in the year."

In the Creator's three forms of cosmic expression, the letter Aleph is like the sound of the spoken word "which cometh of the Air"; Mem is of Water "flowing like the writing of the word"; and Shin is like "the counting of a number which burneth of Fire." Significantly on our planet Earth, Air feeds Fire, and Water extinguishes Fire.

The *three mother letters* also shape the human body, male and female. The head is formed from Fire (Shin), the belly from Water (Mem), the chest from Air (Aleph); and, again, the chest is the link and mediator between head and belly. In the male, the triune sequence is Air-Water-Fire, and in the female Air-Fire-Water. Is it not amazing what a fundamental difference a slight change in the triune sequence can make?

It is especially interesting, though not at all surprising, that the three mother letters form the first word in the Jewish Confession of Faith called the *Shema*. Though not strictly a prayer, it is a vital part of the daily liturgy. Referred to three times in the Old Testament (Deuteronomy 6:4-9 and 11:13-21, and Numbers 15:37-41), the words are: "Hear O Israel, the Lord our God is one Lord." In Hebrew the word "hear" is *Shema* which spells *Sh*(in) - *M* (em) - *A*(leph).

The *seven double letters* (the heptad of Beth, Gimel, Daleth, Kaph, Pe, Resh and Tav) represent changeable forces. They are so named because, depending on their position at the beginning or end of a word, their sound may be hard or soft, aspirated or unaspirated, strong or weak. Each letter has two meanings and illustrates one of the fundamental opposites that humankind must constantly face: life/death, peace/war, wisdom/folly, wealth/poverty, beauty/ugliness, fertility/devastation, and dominion/slavery. The double letters refer likewise to the seven days of creation, the seven heavens, the seven continents, and the seven seas. They are also the Seven Gateways (organs of perception in man, male and female): two eyes, two ears, two nostrils, and the mouth. By means of the seven double letters, there are seven planets (Saturn, Jupiter, Mars, Sun, Venus, Mercury and Moon) to mark the rhythmic heartbeat of the universe in what we call time.

The *twelve simple letters* (the dodecad of He, Vav, Zayin, Cheth, Teth, Yod, Lamed, Nun, Samekh, Ayin, Sadi and Koph) are constant forces, equal in strength and single in sound; yet they stand in constant strife, as if in the order of battle. They personify the twelve tribes of Israel and the twelve months of the Hebrew calendical year. More importantly, they serve as the Arms of the Universe to reach into the infinity of space in twelve directions from which the twelve zodiacal signs proceed (Aries, Taurus, Gemini, Cancer, Leo, Virgo, Libra, Scorpio, Sagittarius, Capricorn, Aquarius and Pisces).

While the twelve simple letters themselves (like the spaces of the zodiac) do not change, they can influence and change the seven double letters (the planets).

In humans the twelve simple letters are the foundation of sight, hearing, smell, speech, taste, sexual love, work (action), movement (motion), wrath, mirth, meditation and sleep; and likewise twelve parts: two hands, two feet, two kidneys, liver, spleen, gall, stomach, colon and bowels.

To seal the *Six Directions of Sacred Space* (*The Book of Formation* I:13), the Lord God chose three Simple letters and put them in his great name, YHVH. From these three letters, called the Trigrammaton, infinite directions extend along three axes:

Figure 27. Sacred Space (Sealed in Six Directions)

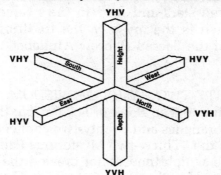

height and depth, east and west, and north and south (Figure 27).

"He sealed the Height stretched upwards . . . with YHV. He sealed the Depth stretched downwards . . . with YVH. He sealed the East stretched forwards . . . with HYV. He sealed the West stretched backwards . . . with HVY. He sealed the North stretched to the right . . . with VYH. He sealed the South stretched to the left . . . with VHY." Some translations of *The Book of Formation* erroneously reverse the last two seals by naming VYH for south and VHY for north.

The Hebrew letter Yod signifies a hand, He signifies a window, and Vav signifies a nail. With regard to sacred space, the letters YHV symbolize the trinity, in which Yod is the supernal father, He the supernal mother, and Vav the son. HVY (the imperative form of the verb "to be") means "be thou." HYV is the infinitive form, and VYH is the future.

In the closing words (Chapter VI) of *The Book of Formation*: "He, the Holy One, bound the twenty-two letters . . . to his tongue. . . . He let them soak in Water, burn in Fire, and sway in the Air. He let them shine in the seven stars and lead in the twelve zodiacal signs." Such is the mystery, the tradition and the message of the Sacred Hebrew Alphabet.

THE THIRTY-TWO PATHS OF WISDOM

According to *The Book of Formation*, the Tree of Life's ten branches and twenty-two connecting paths constitute the "Thirty-two Mysterious Paths of Wisdom" with which the Creator created the universe. The ten Tree branches contain in themselves *also* the first ten paths of wisdom, and the twenty-two alphabet letters are also two-way channels of communication. The Tree branches (numbers one to ten) are natural forces and the substance of creation, creative spheres of causation referring to both universe and humanity. On the other hand, the twenty-two paths (numbers eleven to thirty-two) are states of consciousness and, at the same time, the effects of that creation. By assuming the characteristics of the Tree branches they join, the paths point to externalized relationships existing between the universe and humankind. They also contain psychological messages by which people can expand their awareness of the universe within and around themselves.

Each Hebrew letter has its own sphere of action in a connecting path between two Tree branches. However, the alphabet is not found in chronological order on the Tree of Life, and therefore does not follow the sequence of its numerical values. In our time, this fact applies also to the twenty-two major arcana (trump cards) of the traditional tarot deck, in which several independent systems correspond roughly to both the order of paths and the Hebrew letters.[15] It is said that, in times long passed, both the Tree of Life and the esoteric tarot were essentially "identical twins presented in different garbs."

In placing the signs and symbols on the paths of the Tree of Life, this book follows the simple and logical method of my Teacher. As illustrated in Figure 28, he found the three mother letters with their corresponding elements Air, Water and Fire to belong in paths 11, 12, and 13. (Obviously, the fourth element, Earth, manifests only in the last Tree

Figure 28. The Thirty-Two Paths of Wisdom
(Letters, Elements, Planets & Zodiac Signs)

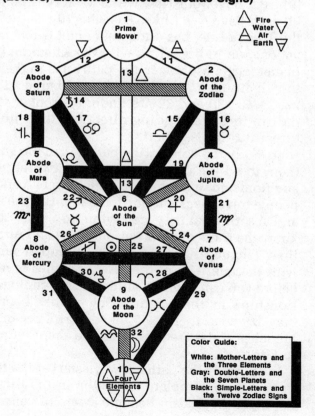

branch.) Likewise he found the seven double letters with their respective planets to belong in paths 14, 20, 22, 24, 25, 26 and 32. Finally he found the twelve simple letters with their complementary twelve zodiacal signs to belong in paths 15, 16, 17, 18, 19, 21, 23, 27, 28, 29, 30 and 31.

As shown in Figure 28, the thirty-two Paths of Wisdom do not all have the same number of connecting paths. The Crown (1) and the Kingdom (10) each have three connecting paths. Wisdom (2), Understanding (3), Mercy (4), Severity (5) and Foundation (9) each have four ties, while Victory (7) and Glory (8) each have five links. The King (6), as the heart of the Tree of Life, has altogether eight direct contacts; yet only an indirect link with the Kingdom (10), our planet Earth. Moreover, the pathways in the route of the Lightning Flash (Figure 5) numbered 11, 14, 19, 22, 24, 27, 30 and 32 are under a stronger vibratory pull in their descending direction; their number of direct ties is also eight.

To study the connecting paths, imagine any one of them to be the only road between two cities (Paris and Rome, for example) on which French and Italian people travel back and forth. To identify the travelers and absorb what they are saying, you must obviously know the traits of their nationalities and understand their languages. That is why thorough familiarity with the qualities of the Tree branches is necessary before you can begin to study the psychological relationships in their connecting paths. Therefore, it may be wise to reread the description of the ten branches of the Tree of Life in the chapter *From Light to Life*.

In studying the paths, always start at the top of the Tree and contemplate the paths in the direction of the Lightning Flash. Become aware of your personal reactions and feelings about them. Always pursue the reverse flow as well. For example, after you have viewed path eleven from the Crown to Wisdom, contemplate it *also* from Wisdom to the Crown.

In contemplating the Thirty-Two Paths of Wisdom (Figure 28) you will notice that:

1. The paths of the planets and double letters either follow or precede their respective planets' abode in the Tree of Life. For example, Path 14 as the working sphere of Saturn and of a double letter precedes the third Tree branch, which is Saturn's home.

To clarify a question concerning different meanings of the seven planets in the Tree branches numbers three to nine and in the seven respective paths: *each Tree branch is a planet's abode and its sphere of influence and life, while each path indicates its space of action and relationships.* It is as though you live in the suburbs while your daily physical presence is in the city. In other words, your home is comparable to the planet's Tree branch whereas your work and your relationships take place on the path of the planet.

2. The paths of the zodiacal signs and the simple letters are closely linked to all Tree branches except for Number 1. This is because the divided space of the zodiac (situated in the Tree branch Number 2) is but a reflection of the undivided space in Number 1.

3. Two of the three mother letters dwelling in paths 11 and 12 connect the Worlds of Origination and Creation. However, Path 13 (the third mother letter) connects the Godhead (Number 1) with the heart of the Tree of Life (Number 6). This is the path on which the Son of God becomes the Son of Man, and the Son of Man becomes again the Son of God.

As to each individual path, the colors indicated are those suggested by my Teacher. They can be used to color your own pictograph.

On the Tree of Life the *11th Path* (color: luminous golden-white) follows the path of the Lightning Flash. Called the Fiery or Scintillating Intelligence, it connects the Crown with Wisdom and links the Pillar of Mildness with Mercy and, in the Supernal Triangle, connects the Godhead to creative maleness. It may be advisable to review these principles in Chapter 8, *Trinity: The Architect of Creation.* To this path is assigned the first mother letter, Aleph, which reigns in the element Air.

The *12th Path* (color: golden yellow) is called the Intelligence of Transparency, also Intelligence of Light. It links the Crown of the Creator with Understanding, and forms the bridge between the Pillars of Mildness and Severity. In the Supernal Triangle, it conjoins the Godhead to the feminine. Those familiar with Goethe's *Faust* will recall the eternal woman who pleads with God for Faust's final salvation in heaven. To this path is assigned the second mother letter, Mem, which reigns in the element Water.

The *13th Path* (color: blue) is called the Conductive Intelligence of Unity, or Uniting Intelligence. It connects the Crown with Beauty the King in the Pillar of Mildness, and links the uniting beams of the Supernal and Ethical Triangles. To this path is assigned the third mother letter Shin which reigns in the element Fire.

The 13th Path in reverse (from the King to the Crown) can be followed by only a very few highly evolved souls who have already attained the vision of the Creator in Christ consciousness or Buddha consciousness.

The *14th Path* (color: green) is within the path of the Lightning Flash. It is called the Luminous or Illuminating Intelligence, and connects Wisdom and

Understanding with the Pillars of Mercy and Severity. It is the Path from the masculine to the feminine, from creative to receptive energy vibrations. To this path are assigned a double letter and the planet Saturn, which resides in the third Tree branch.

The *15th Path* (color: crimson) is called the Constituting Intelligence and connects Wisdom and Beauty the King. It links the Pillars of Mercy and Mildness, and connects the positive base angle of the Supernal Triangle with the uniting beam of the Ethical Triangle. To this path are assigned a simple letter and the zodiacal sign of Libra.

The *16th Path* (color: red-orange) is called the Eternal or Triumphant Intelligence. It connects Wisdom and Mercy—both in the Pillar of Mercy—with the two positive base angles, one being in the Supernal and the other in the Ethical Triangle. To this path are assigned a simple letter and the zodiacal sign of Taurus.

The *17th Path* (color: orange) is called the Sensible and Disposing Intelligence, and connects Understanding with Beauty the King. It joins the Pillar of Severity with that of Mildness, and links the negative base angle of the Supernal Triangle with the uniting beam of the Ethical Triangle. To this path are assigned a simple letter and the zodiacal sign of Cancer.

The *18th Path* (color: yellow-orange) is called the Emanative Intelligence or House of Influence. It connects Understanding and Severity, both in the Pillar of Severity. It links the negative base angle of the Supernal Triangle with that of the Ethical Triangle. To this path are assigned a simple letter and the zodiacal sign of Gemini.

The *19th Path* (color: golden yellow) is within the path of the Lightning Flash, and is called the Intelli-

gence of the Secret of Spiritual Activities. It connects
the two base angles of the Ethical Triangle: Mercy
and Severity (abundance and restriction). It also
joins the Pillars of Mercy and Severity. To this path
are assigned a simple letter and the zodiacal sign of
Leo.

The *20th Path* (color: green) is called the Intelligence of Will and connects Mercy with Beauty the
King. It links the Pillars of Mercy and Mildness, and
the positive base angle with the uniting beam of the
Ethical Triangle. To this path are assigned a double
letter and the planet Jupiter, which resides in the
fourth Tree branch.

The *21st Path* (color: violet) is called the Intelligence of Desire or the Rewarding Intelligence. It connects Mercy and Victory, both in the Pillar of Mercy.
It also links the positive base angles of the Ethical
and Astral Triangles. To this path are assigned a simple letter and the zodiacal sign of Virgo.

The *22nd Path* (color: green) is within the path of
the Lightning Flash. It is called the Faithful Intelligence and connects Severity with Beauty the King. It
links the Pillar of Severity with the Pillar of Mildness, and the negative base angle with the uniting
beam of the Ethical Triangle. To this path are assigned a double letter and the planet Mars, which
resides in the fifth Tree branch.

The *23rd Path* (color: blue) is called the Stable
Intelligence and connects Strength and Glory, both
in the Pillar of Severity. It also links two negative
base angles, one of the Ethical, the other of the Astral
Triangle. To this path are assigned a simple letter and
the zodiacal sign of Scorpio.

The *24th Path* (color: blue-green) is within the
Path of the Lightning Flash. It is called the Imaginative Intelligence, and connects Beauty the King and

Victory, as well as the Pillar of Mildness with the Pillar of Mercy. It also links the uniting beam of the Ethical Triangle to the positive base angle of the Astral Triangle. To this path are assigned a double letter and the planet Venus, which resides in the seventh Tree branch.

The *25th Path* (color: blue) crosses the Veil of Paroketh. It is called the Intelligence of Temptation, Trial or Probation and connects Beauty the King with the Foundation, both in the Pillar of Mildness. It links two uniting beams, one in the Ethical, the other in the Astral Triangle. To this path are assigned a double letter and the sun, which resides in the sixth Tree branch.

The *26th Path* (color: blue-violet) is called the Renewing Intelligence and connects Beauty the King with Glory. It links the Pillar of Mildness to the Pillar of Severity, and connects the uniting beam of the Ethical Triangle with the negative base angle of the Magical Triangle. To this path are assigned a double letter and the planet Mercury, which resides in the eighth Tree branch.

The *27th Path* (color: red) is within the Path of the Lightning Flash. It is called the Natural or Exciting Intelligence, and connects Victory (feeling) and Glory (thinking). It also links the Pillars of Mercy and Severity and ties the two base angles of the Astral Triangle. To this path are assigned a simple letter and the zodiacal sign of Sagittarius.

The *28th Path* (color: violet) is called the Palpable or Active Intelligence. It connects Victory and the Foundation, and the Pillar of Mercy with the Pillar of Mildness. It also links both the positive base angle and the uniting beam of the Moral Triangle. To this path are assigned a simple letter and the zodiacal sign of Aries.

The *29th Path* (color: rose-red) is called the Corporeal Intelligence and connects Victory with the Kingdom, as well as the Pillars of Mercy and Mildness. It also links the positive base angle of the Astral Triangle with the Kingdom. To it are assigned a simple letter and the zodiacal sign of Pisces.

The *30th Path* (color: orange) is within the path of the Lightning Flash. It is called the Collective Intelligence and connects Glory (of the Mind) with the Foundation. It ties the Pillar of Severity to that of Mildness, and the negative base angle to the uniting beam of the Astral Triangle. To this path are assigned a simple letter and the zodiacal sign of Capricorn.

The *31st Path* (color: red) is called the Perpetual Intelligence and connects Glory (of the Mind) and the Kingdom. It ties the Pillar of Severity and of Mildness, and the negative base angle of the Astral Triangle to the Kingdom. To this path are assigned a simple letter and the zodiacal sign of Aquarius.

The *32nd Path* (color: blue-violet) is within the path of the Lightning Flash. It is called the Assisting Intelligence and connects the Foundation and the Kingdom, both in the Pillar of Mildness. Assigned to this path is the double letter Tav (meaning "cross"), which refers to the equal-armed solar cross of the four Elements of Life in the Kingdom. To it is also attributed the moon, which resides in the ninth Tree branch.

According to legend the Priestess of the Silver Star sits in the Kingdom at the Footstool of God, ready to guide all seekers of truth from the darkness of terrestrial life into the light of freedom.

Space tells matter how to move, and matter tells space how to curve.

Einstein

The Piscean Age made Divinity human; the Aquarian Age will make Humanity Divine.

William Gray

11
Kabbalistic Astrology: Yardsticks in the Sky: Restless Time in Endless Space

There are many more stars in the skies than grains of sand on the shores of the seven seas, and, it would seem, more professional astrologers in today's industrialized world than practicing physicians and psychologists combined. Astrological counseling continues at a healthy rate with faithful clients from all walks of life.

Classical astrology (the logic of the stars) interprets and predicts relationships between the stars (the macrocosm) and humans (the microcosm). Stellar and planetary distances, angles and patterns in the firmament are measured by the astrologer and compared with planetary configurations in the natal chart. Finally their import on future events is interpreted and forecast.

Figure 29. The Wheel of the Zodiac (Summary)

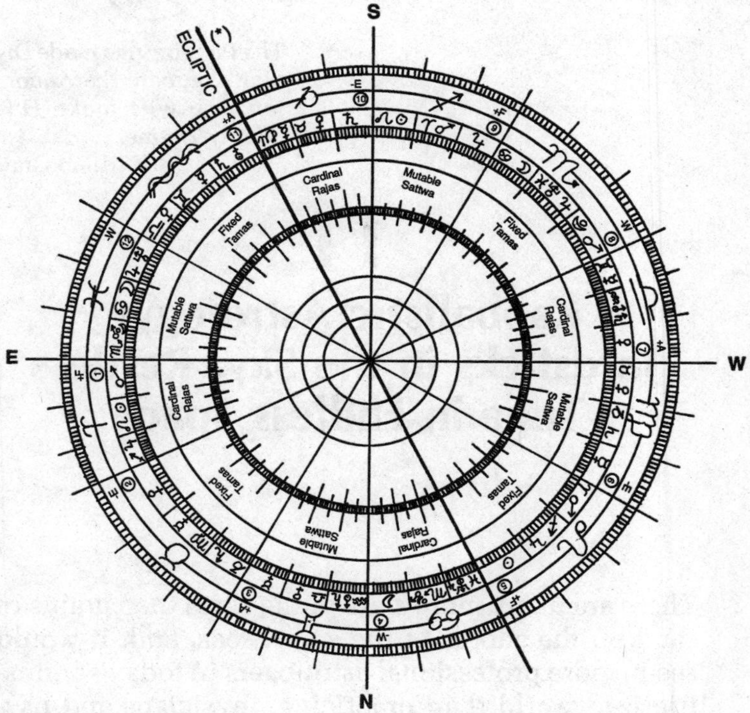

*) ecliptic: dealing with earth orbit, about 23.½°

E, S, W and N: geographic directions, east, west, south and north

1, 4, 7, 10 (cardinal)
2, 5, 8, 11 (fixed)   quadriplicities
3, 6, 9, 12 (movable)

Numbers 1 to 12: of zodiac sign or house

+ and −: consecutive positive and negative opposites

F, E, A and W: the four triplicities, Fire, Earth, Air and Water

Classical astrology has been event oriented (Figure 29) and time conditioned ever since the golden days of the learned Babylonians and Chaldeans. Because God himself had placed the sun, the moon and the planets in the firmament as signs and seasons (Genesis 1:14), these ancient people observed the star-studded sky to "read" the Creator's secret plans for the future of humanity.

Kabbalistic astrology investigates the psychological projection of an individual into the zodiac and the planets which abide in the branches of the Tree of Life (Figure 30). Based on one's place and moment of birth it demonstrates why and how the universe and the human being are like the two sides of one coin. It illustrates the evolution of humanity in relation to the immediate environment *and* that of the universe as viewed from our planet Earth (Figure 28).

Kabbalistic astrology may thus be defined as the time-and-speed-measured, firmament-projected cosmic drama of a threefold angular relationship among three "acting heroes" on the stage of life. The first is

Figure 30. The Tree of Life:
The Abode of Zodiac and Planets

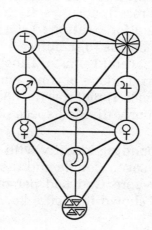

Figure 31. Angular Relationships

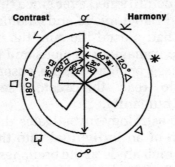

the life force in perpetual motion; the second the confining time of the wandering planets; and the third is the expanding space of the belt of the zodiac.

These three courageous actors, which are constantly changing, impress and influence each other and each person. They are sometimes in harmony and sometimes in contrast or conflict (Figure 31), depending on the actual distances or the angles which unite or separate them.

The system of Western astrology is strongly associated with certain numbers. An intimate kinship between the numbers seven and twelve is not surprising, for both result from the numbers three and four. Three, you will recall, portrays divine completeness as the foundation for creation to start, while in four actual creation begins to manifest.

The number seven (3 plus 4) illustrates the traditional planets as markers of time, whereas the number twelve (3 times 4) pictures the 360-degree zodiacal circle as orderly divided space (360 = 3 x 10 x 12).

Their corresponding identity with the Hebrew alphabet, via the seven double and the twelve simple letters that the Lord God had personally designed and sealed, are shown in Figure 26.

THE ZODIAC

The story of life begins in space. Just as the ten branches of the Tree of Life illustrate definite universal qualities, so the twelve equal-sized arcs of the zodiac—like the twelve labors of Hercules—symbolize successive stages of human metaphysical evolution. In numerical sequence from one to twelve, each 30-degree sector (called a "house" by astrologers) is the home of one sign of the zodiac. Each personifies one quality or activity which one must experience on the way to perfection. On the Tree of Life the name of the mythical being is Adam Kadmon.

There is much to tell about the zodiacal wheel. Each sector illustrates both space and time; each has one ruling planet, and sometimes two, whose qualities blend naturally with the characteristics of its zodiacal sign.

Figure 32. The Rose of Heaven
(Planetary Rulers)

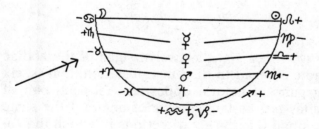

Zodiacal Groupings

Because of its symmetrical design, the twelve-spoked wheel of the zodiac divides into four different numerical groupings. They can be viewed as 6 times the number 2, 2 times the number 6, 4 times the number 3, or 3 times the number 4.

As *six times two,* and starting with a positive

sign,* we may view the zodiac as six *consecutive* pairs of opposites. You may call them positive and negative, male and female, or active and passive. Alternating six times between a positive, electric, and masculine and a negative, magnetic radiating and feminine polarity, a positive, masculine sign is always followed by a negative, feminine one. It is as though each consecutive sign would react against its forerunner (see Figure 33 for a visual presentation). Notice that all feminine signs are even numbered, and all masculine signs are odd numbered.

Figure 33. The "Six Times Two" in the Zodiac

As *two times six*, the twelve signs of the zodiac illustrate a hexad in dual manifestation, that is, six facing pairs of natural opposites. Yet each pair of opposites is like two aspects of one and the same thing, much like the six directions in which the Tetragrammaton was sealed.

In this grouping, the first six signs present what one has to learn, and the second six what is to be shared with one's fellows. Table 5 shows what this

---

*The positive signs are Aries, Gemini, Leo, Libra, Sagittarius and Aquarius. The negative signs are Taurus, Cancer, Virgo, Scorpio, Capricorn and Pisces.

Table 5

THE "TWO TIMES SIX"
IN
THE ZODIAC

What's to Learn?

No.	Sign	Ruler	In Manifestation	In Evolution
1	Aries	♂	dynamic energy	aspiration
2	Taurus	♀	steadfast action in matter	integration
3	Gemini	☿	the searching mind	vivifaction
4	Cancer	☽	emotion; means to hold on to one's own authority	self-expansion
5	Leo	☉	determination	assurance
6	Virgo	☿	digestion of matter	discrimination; assimilation

What's to Share?

No.	Sign	Ruler	In Manifestation	In Evolution
7	Libra	♀	intuition	balance
8	Scorpio	♂	goal direction	creativity
9	Sagittarius	♃	inspiration	universal awareness; illumination
10	Capricorn	♄	action in matter	organization
11	Aquarius	♄	intuition; destroys and builds structure	originality; loyalty
12	Pisces	♃	compassion; gives birth to the perfected man	sacrifice; selfless giving

entails in both manifestation and evolution. What one has learned in Aries can be evaluated and balanced in Libra. What has been embodied in Taurus can be recreated in Scorpio. What has been thought in Gemini can be clearly seen in Sagittarius. What has been felt in Cancer can be used indiscriminately in Capricorn. What has been willed in Leo can be know in Aquarius; and what has been analyzed in Virgo can be believed and sacrificed in Pisces.

As *four times three*, the twelve zodiacal signs present four triangular patterns of unilateral (120-degree) angles and represent the four fundamental Elements of Life: Fire, Earth, Air and Water (Table 6). These four Elements are not only the cradle of all metaphysical thought (including astrology) but also illustrate the four states of matter—Fire as primary energy, Earth as solid, Air as gaseous and Water as liquid. Each of the four Elements is expressed in three different qualities, called the triplicities.

On the plane of action each triplicity illustrates a level of consciousness, progression or action. Fire corresponds to divine will in action, Earth to thought assimilated in action, Air to mental awareness, and Water to receptivity of feelings.

Table 7 shows how each triplicity manifests on the plane of existence: Fire as inspiration, Earth as action in matter, Air as intuition and aspiration, and Water as emotion.

In an individual horoscope, fire signs denote leadership: people who have Fire signs are determined, ardent, strong willed and active. Earth signs denote achievement: people with Earth signs are practical, thorough and introverted. Air signs denote independence: people who have Air signs are intuitive, expressive and extroverted. Water signs denote under-

Table 6

THE FOUR ELEMENTS OF LIFE
in
THE ZODIAC

Plane of Action — The Four Elements	Divine Will in Action — FIRE	Expression and Assimilation — EARTH	Inner Awareness — AIR	Receptivity of Feelings — WATER
	m ♈ ♂ — ARIES — 1	f ♉ ♀ — TAURUS — 2	m ♊ ☿ — GEMINI — 3	f ♋ ☽ — CANCER — 4
	m ♌ ☉ — LEO — 5	f ♍ ☿ — VIRGO — 6	m ♎ ♀ — LIBRA — 7	f ♏ ♂ — SCORPIO — 8
	m ♐ ♃ — SAGITTARIOUS — 9	f ♑ ♄ — CAPRICORN — 10	m ♒ ♄ — AQUARIUS — 11	f ♓ ♃ — PISCES — 12
Plane of Existence — Manifestation	INSPIRATION — MIND	MATTER in ACTION	ASPIRATION — INTUITION	EMOTION

Note: upper left corner: m=male (positive); f=female (negative)
     upper right corner: the rulers
     lower right corner: numerical value of sign

Table 7

THE FOUR TRIPLICITIES
IN
THE ZODIAC

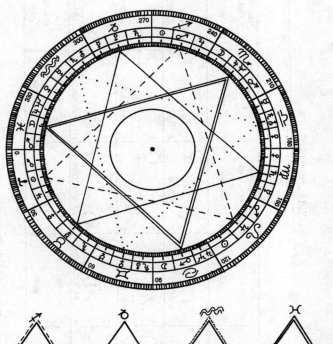

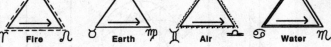

Fire   Earth   Air   Water

standing: people with Water signs are emotional, intuitive, mystical and preserving.

By analogy, in the Tao all Fire and Air signs are Yang (active, outgoing and self-expressive); all Earth and Water signs are Yin (passive, responsive and receptive).

Lastly, let us look at the twelve zodiacal signs as *three times four* (Table 8). Called quadruplicities, these three groups of four describe cycles or modes of action and expression in the plane of evolution, in contradistinction to the four triplicities which, as we have just witnessed, illustrate the plane of action and the plane of existence. Sometimes the quadruplicities are labeled active, passive and balancing. They show *how* things happen in accordance with the Elements of Life: firstly as qualities of action in the cardinal or movable signs; secondly as stability or reaction in the fixed signs; thirdly, and finally, as rhythm of interaction and beginning indications of changes in the mutable or common signs.

Some astrologers use Sanskrit words for the three groups of four to identify the three *gunas*: *rajas* for the positive and expanding, *tamas* for the negative and contracting, and *sattwa* for the harmonizing and uniting qualities. On the three levels of human temperament, rajas is the impulsive birth of a thing, tamas its life, and sattwa its passing over. In fact you may look at the three gunas as physical manifestations of the same thing, like liquid water, solid ice and volatile water vapor.

The four cardinal or movable signs (Aries, Cancer, Libra and Capricorn) signify rajas. They are pioneering, impulsive, ambitious, action-oriented, outgoing and restless by desire. The four fixed signs (Taurus,

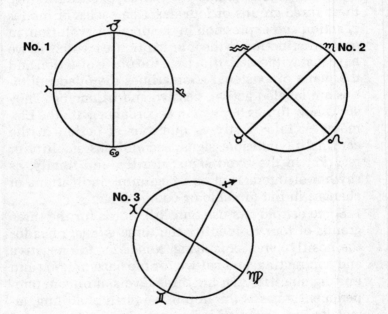

Table 8

<u>THE QUADRIPLICITIES</u>
<u>IN</u>
<u>THE ZODIAC</u>

Three circles with four signs each: in opposition
(180 degrees apart) and in squares (90 degrees apart)

No. 1

No. 2

No. 3

Number 1: cardinal or movable signs, representing <u>rajas</u>

Number 2: fixed signs, corresponding to <u>tamas</u>

Number 3: mutable or common signs belonging to <u>sattwa</u>

Table 9

ACTION AND EXPRESSION OF THE FOUR ELEMENTS

Sign: Quality: Plane of Evolution: Name:	Plane of Existence: ELEMENT:	CARDINAL or MOVABLE expanding (active) quality of action RAJAS "Pioneers"	No.	FIXED contracting (passive) stability or reaction TAMAS "Perfectors"	No.	MUTABLE or COMMON uniting (balancing) interaction SATTWA "Developers"	No.
Fire △ action: divine will existence: inspiration	primary energy	Aries ♈ will for action: initiates	1	Leo ♌ assurance: wills	5	Sagittarius ♐ administration: sees	9
Earth ▽ action: thought in action existence: action in matter	solid	Capricorn ♑ discrimination: uses	10	Taurus ♉ stability: integrates	2	Virgo ♍ assimilation: analyzes	6
Air △ action: mental awareness existence: intuition, aspiration	gaseous	Libra ♎ balance: evaluates	7	Aquarius ♒ loyalty: knows	11	Gemini ♊ versatility: thinks	3
Water ▽ action: feelings existence: emotion	liquid	Cancer ♋ expansion: permeates	4	Scorpio ♏ creativity: desires	8	Pisces ♓ devotion: sacrifices	12
MANIFESTATION:		initiating		persistent		adapting	

The Four States of Matter.

Leo, Scorpio and Aquarius) are perfectors and signify tamas. They are passive, inflexible, concentrated, and exert inertia and stagnation in everything that is undertaken; they also indicate an attitude of conservative stability. The four mutable or common signs (Gemini, Virgo, Sagittarius and Pisces) signify sattwa. They are the developers. Whatever they achieve is to be held in balance; they are flexible, versatile, adaptable and harbor a strong desire for harmony and change.

THE PLANETS

Space (the zodiac) needs time to manifest, and time (the planets) needs space to act. As the planets travel through the twelve arcs of space they reveal themselves in our consciousness. Thus, only in the cradle of space can time sing its melodies. This is why Pythagoras called astrology the "music of the spheres." To the great sage this was no poetic figure of speech but rather an attempt to provide a practical definition for identical mathematical ratios between musical intervals and the planetary distances (see Table 2).

As they move through space, the planets leave no footprints, neither do they ever collide with one another, even though their moving pattern and pace differ greatly. For instance, it takes the sun one month to move through one zodiacal sign, while the moon travels through all twelve in less than twenty-eight days.

With all this constant planetary travel, the spatial relationships within the zodiac do not change. But they do indeed change the life expression and the mode of action of the planets that pass through them.

The Planetary Symbols Clarified

The actual design of the planetary symbols deepens our understanding of the planets as they reside in the Tree of Life and as "markers of time" in astrology. There is an intimate kinship (if not an outright character identity) between the two. (Table 1, and Figures 26 and 28).

The pictorial design of the so-called seven "traditional" planets follows three universal patterns: the circle, the half-circle and the cross. The actual placement of these patterns in each symbol tells much about its planet's outstanding qualities.

The *circle*, a line with no beginning or end, pictures creation in its infinity and unity. Situated in the Tree of Life's first branch, it illustrates eternal selfness without otherness in whatever has been, is, and ever shall be.

The *circle with a central point* represents the one undivided origin of manifest life with the cosmic seed in its center. It is therefore the astrological symbol of the luminary Sun as the only direct and permanent light-energy source of our planet Earth. Consequently, the Sun has its prominent place in the very heart of the Tree of Life, which is its sixth branch.

By drawing a vertical line through the circle's central point, two *mirror-fashioned half-circles* disclose the polarity of life. These half-circles are the symbol of the perpetually waxing and waning Moon. On the Tree of Life the Moon abides in its ninth branch,

where physical duality consistently separates and
reunites the rhythmic ebb and flow of life as time
measured in endless space, and the terrestrial sexuality of humankind as male and female.

With a straight horizontal line drawn through the
vertically divided circle, the *cross within the circle*
appears. It illustrates the Four Elements of Life
which reside in the Tree's tenth and last branch.

There is more to the cross within the circle. In the
skies it indicates two pairs of turning points: (1) the
spring and fall equinoxes when day and night are of
equal length (about March 20 and September 22);
and (2) the summer solstice or longest day and winter solstice as longest night (about June 22 and De-
cember 22).

By cutting windows at the four corners of the cir-
cled cross, another cross appears within the circle in
the Tree's first branch, called the *mystical swastika*.
It is the ever-revolving wheel of change, and also the
turning wheel of the Four Elements of Life. Here is
but one reference to the abiding law "as above so
below."

The *cross without the circle* marks the ancient
equal-armed cross. Called the *solar cross*, it is the
origin of all later world crosses and, as legend tells,

our constant invisible companion on our terrestrial journey. On the Tree of Life, the solar cross is rightfully the pictorial design of its tenth branch where the one from the first branch becomes the many. And yet, in their totality, the many are again as one.

$$+$$

The seven traditional planets are ambiguous in character and can be at once in harmony with and in contrast or conflict to the "lights of day and night." Table 10 illustrates how the solar cross combines with either the Sun or the Moon, and at times with both, to form various quality relationships.

Following the Path of the Lightning Flash, the first and most distant planet is *Saturn*. Its symbolic design places the cross above its inward half-circle. It reveals a compressing, self-limiting and restraining power of endurance, self-preservation and stabilization, and is representative of the receptive feminine and the conservative realist.

$$\textrm{ℏ}$$

The symbol of the planet *Jupiter*, on the other hand, carries a half-circle (the crescent moon) sideways above its cross. It shows how, in life, expanding powers govern and integrate progressive development with the strong will to live and share, and thereby describes the compassionate masculine side of life and generous idealistic behavior.

$$\textrm{♃}$$

Table 10

RELATIONSHIPS BETWEEN PLANETARY SYMBOLS

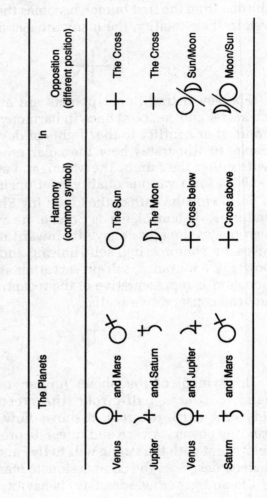

The Planets	In Harmony (common symbol)	Opposition (different position)
Venus ♀ and Mars ♂	○ The Sun	+ The Cross
Jupiter ♃ and Saturn ♄	☽ The Moon	+ The Cross
Venus ♀ and Jupiter ♃	+ Cross below	⊙/☽ Sun/Moon
Saturn ♄ and Mars ♂	+ Cross above	☽/⊙ Moon/Sun

The symbolic design of the planet *Mars* is a cross pointing sideways on a circle. Originally the cross was drawn above the circle to indicate that human driving powers dominate and mobilize outer activities. Only at a much later date was the cross moved to its present position, thus pinpointing the planet's masculine, phallic and aggressive qualities.

Next is the *Sun*, the eternal, centralized, creative power and vitalizing spirit. It represents the life-giving warmth and light of manifest existence. The Sun resides in the heart of the Tree of Life, where light becomes radiating love and love becomes life.

The symbol of the planet *Venus* carries a circle above the cross. It illustrates aesthetic completion as well as those spiritual powers necessary to harmonize instincts, desires and physical energies with actions.

The symbol of the planet *Mercury* combines a half-circle with a circle above and a cross below. It personifies the many-faceted mind which, though elusive like quicksilver, can communicate as a messenger between its conscious, subconscious and superconscious levels. As a "mirror of the intellect," it can decide between "good and evil," change thoughts at the spur of the moment, and store gained knowledge as experienced memory.

As the symbol indicates, the dual nature of this planet is both positive *and* negative, active *and* passive, and electric *and* magnetic, with electrical qualities predominating. Thereby, Mercury heralds the duality of life on the planet Earth.

Last on the Path of the Lightning Flash is the second luminary, the *Moon*, illustrating physical and psychic "substance" and responsive ability. Residing in the Tree's ninth branch, the Moon causes a ceaseless interchange between fluidity and solidity, and with it brings to the fore the basis for all "breathing life."

Now to the three planets, discovered in modern times, which were missing in the vision of Pythagoras.

The symbolic design of the planet *Uranus* places the Sun under a cross, and flanks the latter sideways by both a waxing and waning Moon. This image suggests that intuitive powers penetrate and pervade all creative levels, and change suddenly from the unexpected to the expected.

The symbol of the planet *Neptune* places both a waxing and waning Moon above a cross, producing a three-pronged fork design. It illustrates a compassionate longing which acts as a unifier behind the veiled and secret-holding Great Beyond, and is sometimes considered to represent the father-mother-child trinity.

The symbols of the planet *Pluto* have two equally popular designs. One carries the initials of Percival Lowell, the astronomer who, based on the discovery of Uranus in 1781, made calculations that led to its discovery by Peter Tombough in 1930. The second pattern places an empty circle (the emblem of infinity) into the center of the horizontal, moon-like half-circle which, in turn, rests above the cross. Pluto is often called the anti-establishment humanitarian. He is the altruistic purifier and eliminates whatever does not help the community at large. Further research may reveal more of Pluto's kaleidoscopic and often still legendary qualities.

IV
From Life to Light
(Pathway of Progression)

*Love is not Love until it is
given away.*

12
Life's Innermost Secrets: The Story of Daath

Hidden, veiled and protected like the roots of the Tree of Life is a Tree branch with no apparent ties to the others. It holds the mysterious secret of life in its fold, that secret which is in essence the innermost secret of your life. Its name is Daath (Figure 1). Daath is always more than can be said with words. To be understood, its secrets must be experienced.

To know the name of this Tree branch is an important first step. For the Hebrew word *Daath* means knowledge of a special kind. It is knowledge in the biblical sense of Adam knowing Eve, and Eve knowing Adam. Daath is therefore both the outer act and the inner experience of sharing. It is a union in which each part is simultaneously both active and passive in seeking fulfillment.

Viewed from the Earth plane (and from the tenth Tree branch), Daath hangs over an abyss on the border between the Worlds of Creation and Formation. Here is where the soul and the mind touch and share an amicable relationship. Daath also lies between the Tree branches of creative Wisdom and receptive Understanding, and it faces the Crown of the Godhead.

More specifically, Daath represents the intimate relationship between the active and passive creative Wisdom of male energy and active and passive receptive Understanding of female energy. Within this intimacy, the identity of each partner is never lost, much the same as light and darkness meet but do not mingle. Daath means altruistic sharing by giving and receiving; it is a partnership and can never occur in singleness. In short, *Daath is the cradle of relationships.*

The second step reveals Daath within the Laws of Life. For example, its vibration changes direction as it moves within the Law of Change. Moving at its own speed and pattern according to the Law of Rhythm, it is object or subject, active or passive, as it gives or receives in the Laws of Polarity and Opposition.

By being in close proximity to the absolute, Daath is able to know the paradox of two extremes becoming one single wave of awareness. It can experience both happiness and unhappiness, attraction and rejection, and all the pairs of opposites simultaneously. In a human relationship, Daath can even love and fear the same person at the same time.

The third and giant step into Daath unveils the secret of creation in action. With selfless sharing and self-knowledge growing steadily, the Creator's special gift to humankind is born in Daath. It is the personal and individual free will, the ability to accept or reject, to comply or to oppose. The stronger the human will, the better it can kindle and sustain an ardent desire to give back what has been received, to co-create with nature and pro-create with divinity. This creative urge for generation and regeneration is the reason why Daath is often named the Tree branch of Becoming.

The personal free will, desire and motive behind the act of sharing always determine the level of each Daath experience. With inherent power physical love comes to the fore. Thus Daath is the cradle of physical love, for human life has its material beginning in the sex act. Voluntary and joyful sharing is the pass key to the flow of this deepest mystery of creation. All human beings must find their own passage to growing understanding of the mystery of Love.

Love has its own law, and love of the Laws of Life is the Law of Love. Real love knows nothing less than Love itself. Love is of three kinds: of the physical body; of the emotions, which is part of desire and an outward aspect of love; and spiritual, inspired by the quintessence of knowledge attained through wisdom and understanding. If all three kinds of love are joyfully united, then Daath is understood.

Human sexual love also has three levels. The first is innate instinct, supported by subtle chakras and internal glands. On this level a physical need and its appeasement are expressed, thus conveying the greatest feeling of well-being Earth can offer. At the second level of physical love is Eros with all its enthusiasm and excitement, its profound joy and ecstasy in expression. On the third level, physical love is carried on the wings of the love god Eros with an almost painful longing to belong to someone or something. This third level also displays a basic animal quality of sheer gratification of the physical senses.

Plato also embraced the different phases of love from the personal to impersonal feelings. Known as platonic love, and beginning with the ascent of physical love between man and woman as in Daath, the ascent continues gradually through the protective love between parent and child, to the love of a friend, the compassionate love of beauty, the love of the good and the love of wisdom. At the height of its ascent, platonic love is realized as purest love — the inspired love of God.

Have we earned the right to love? Do we know that our love is only as deep as the love we have for the human being we love the least? Do we sense the needs of those we love, and do we fulfill them joyfully? If so, then we have learned the magic — yes, the magic — of love with a capital L. It is love under free will and in harmony with the endless love and will of the Creator. For the totality of Love is the clay of the universe.

The daily personal prayer of St. Francis of Assisi reveals his clear understanding of Daath: "O Lord, my God, make me an instrument of thy love, let me know, let it be now that I earn the right to know, that I earn the right to love, as is thy nature."

13
Thirteen: The Creator's Abode

It has been repeatedly stated that through transcendental unfoldment one can attain cosmic consciousness while still in the physical body. As each human being seeks to find higher knowledge and deeper understanding, his journey is like climbing from the valley in the world of matter, action and need (the tenth branch of the Tree of Life) to the mountain in the world of formation (the sixth Tree branch). As one progresses, the scenery is constantly changing, and the view of a heretofore unseen universe is ever widening.

The following myth will bring welcome hints to the many who are still on their way to cosmic awareness. Those who have already reached their goal may be able to fill in a few missing details.

The myth (Figure 34) is the vision of Adam Kadmon. We have met him already through his role in the zodiacal wheel as the Creator's idea of a perfect human in the individualized universe. Like all citizens of our planet, Adam Kadmon is at home in human consciousness. His feet are well grounded on planet Earth, yet his eyes look into infinite space. Adam Kadmon has reached cosmic consciousness and apprehends the Laws of Life and the secrets of Daath. At the moment of apprehension, he stood in the heart of the Tree of Life. The view from the mountain top looked remarkably different from the view in the valley. Adam Kadmon no longer saw the ten-branched Tree of Harmony and Unity and the Pythagorean Number Ten with its outer teachings. At first, he witnessed a symmetrical twelve-branched "completed" and balanced Tree of Life as a reflection of the atomic structure in the universe.

Figure 34. The Thirteen-Branched Tree of Life

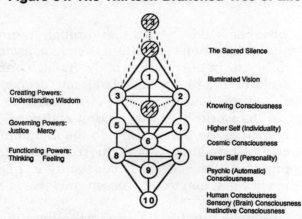

The Sacred Silence

Illuminated Vision

Creating Powers:
Understanding Wisdom

Knowing Consciousness

Governing Powers:
Justice   Mercy

Higher Self (Individuality)

Cosmic Consciousness

Functioning Powers:
Thinking   Feeling

Lower Self (Personality)

Psychic (Automatic)
Consciousness

Human Consciousness
Sensory (Brain) Consciousness
Instinctive Consciousness

How did Adam Kadmon's vision manifest? Starting at the bottom branch of the Tree of Life, he journeyed from human (brain) consciousness through automatic consciousness, and at the same time experienced the spiritual longing of psychic consciousness. Continuing along, he passed through the functional powers of thinking and feeling until he had earned cosmic consciousness. But here, in the heart of the Tree of Life, everything was different.

Formerly hidden, Daath emerged as an eleventh regular Tree branch with its own consciousness of knowing. In the balance of the perfect twelve (the number of governmental completion according to Pythagorean number science) there was a twelfth Tree branch of precosmic substance, partly hidden in Ain Soph Aur. At the point where the Lightning Flash of Creation ignites itself, this twelfth Tree branch with its inner teachings was beyond the Crown (the first Tree branch) and had the power of life that unites and strengthens, creates and sustains its own creation in sacred silence. It was strongly connected with the Crown and with the creating powers of Wisdom and Understanding.

Far beyond the Ain Soph Aur Tree branch was the holy Thirteen, the abode of the Creator. Again, it connected directly with Wisdom and Understanding, and indirectly with the Crown. In Thirteen, the Tree of Life was in equilibrium. Wonders never cease.

Could it be that the author of the harmonious ten-branched Tree of Life left it deliberately incomplete, and unbalanced? Did he perhaps omit it so that humankind would not misunderstand the Holy Thirteen?

Thirteen has been and still is a venerable, if not altogether sacred, number among those who know its transcendental powers. To the Aztecs, Toltecs and the people of Yucatan, the Maya, the number Thirteen was sacred, as were their thirteen snake gods. The original states of the American Union were thirteen. Among observing Jews, the thirteenth birthday marks Bar Mitzvah or Bas Mitzvah for girls, which, in time-honored tradition, makes one an active member of the community. In some Christian traditions, it is the time for first Communion for boys and girls.

It seems that the number thirteen has always been "unprotected by silence." Leaders often appointed twelve followers. Jesus the Nazarene had twelve apostles; counting Jesus, the number was thirteen. King Arthur had twelve knights; at his Round Table thirteen seats were occupied. St. Francis had twelve faithful followers; his first order consisted of thirteen members.

On the other hand, Thirteen tops the lists of the most fearful superstitions. Many hotels and high-rise apartment buildings have no designated thirteenth floor and no room numbered thirteen.

In Adam Kadmon's vision the awareness of Thirteen is joy, not happiness—a joy which has no root in any experience of the five senses, a joy which is the apperception of awakened consciousness. In contradistinction to happiness, which is a fickle and fleeting thing, joy on the terrestrial level is our primary reality. It is not affected by external matters, nor is it dependent on any thing or any person. Once joy has come into your life, it is there to stay.

Says Adam Kadmon: "With thirteen branches on the Tree of Life, the universe is the noisy container for the silent Creator. Accordingly, the ultimate goal of humanity is beyond realization. As love is the fulfillment of the Law, it is service to the Creator and to the Creator's humanity. It is creativity."

"... And on either side of the river, was there the Tree of Life, which bare twelve manner of fruits, and yielded her fruit every month; and the leaves of the fruit were for the healing of all nations."

Revelation 22:2

14
Harvest From the Tree of Life
(Practical Pointers)

What you don't use, you lose. The more you prune the branches of the tree, the more will it bear good fruit. And the more familiar you become with the Tree of Life, the more it will reveal its secrets about the world around you. Your desire to learn must be strong and persistent, but you still need a technique for the constructive study of the Tree of Life.

First some pointers which are easier to follow than to describe. You will find them helpful if used regularly and frequently.

To experience the Tree of Life, apply its wisdom to your daily activities.

Observe joyfully and persistently. The greatest teacher is observation. To become an active observer, take three steps in sequence. First, observe without doubt or prejudice. Then, become an unbiased witness of what you have observed. Finally, apply and experience what you have learned.

Be patient. Rushing always hinders, and tension

spoils progress. The danger of speed is fanaticism. Speed invites shallowness. Remember, patience is another word for perseverance.

Take one step at a time. Make haste slowly. As a steady fall of water — one drop at a time — hollows out a heavy stone, so can you overcome the obstacles of everyday life by moving ahead just one step at a time.

Be alert. Discard personal opinions. Meet the new without struggle. Since change never comes easily, keep your desire for progress strong. Enthusiasm without desire turns easily into anxiety, and much is lost. Choose your goal with care because you always walk in the direction in which you look.

Listen to your heart. Do not simply accept everything you hear. He who lives by a crystal ball ends up eating broken glass.

Set aside time for study and meditation. Regular concentration, meditation and contemplation will prove most beneficial in your study of the Tree of Life. Plan your time daily or weekly to fit your life style. Choose a time when you are not going to be disturbed or interrupted. Early morning and evening hours seem to be good times for many. If the demands of the world sometimes interfere, stick as closely as you can to your chosen schedule without being rigid or feeling guilty.

Recognize the difference between work and labor. Labor is a means to an end. Often a necessity for economic survival, it is mostly an expenditure of energy. Work, on the other hand, is a collaboration between heart and mind for a self-chosen reason and a definite purpose. Wisely executed, work is always revitalizing; it makes and keeps you free. A yardstick for knowing which is which measures work which satisfies and makes you stronger against labor which is tiring and often boring.

The Universe and You

Since the Tree of Life illustrates both the objective universe and the subjective you, there are, as already mentioned, two ways to view its branches.

To study the universe around you, look straight at the Tree (Figure 1). To observe yourself as the mirror image of the universe, look at the Three Pillars of Manifest Harmony (Figure 20). It is important to turn your back mentally into the pictograph so that your spine remains in the center Pillar of Mildness, while your right arm and leg become the Pillar of Severity, and your left arm and leg the Pillar of Mercy.

Then, in a transcendental sense, the hand of the microcosm matches the hand of the macrocosm front to front just as when you put the palm of your hand toward a mirror, the reflected hand matches yours.

A *moment of gathering forces* is recommended as concentration before actual study or meditation.

1. *Surround yourself with a mantle of silence.* You may want to say a few words of invocation, either your own or the following: "In the name of the creative power which works in silence, and which naught but the silence can comprehend, I enter the silence."

2. *Empty yourself.* It is important to clear your mind's vessel of the old and stale, in order to be filled with the fresh and new. A few deep exhalations will accomplish it. A mental picture of a full cup of water which slowly empties itself will also help.

3. *Listen to your own silence*; it is always louder than words and sound.

There are two ways to meditate and each has a different goal. One embraces the events of your life;

the other focuses on the Tree of Life. For a detailed description, see the end of this chapter. Also, note the distinctions between concentration, meditation and contemplation.

Both concentration and meditation are faculties of the mind. Concentration is the necessary first step in training the mind for meditation and requires positive or active control of the mind. Meditation allows the mind to enter its passive or receptive state.

Concentration focuses your attention. The mind needs to be alert, positive, forceful and in an attitude of command. Concentration narrows the field of your attention for a time determined by your will. Its purpose is to form and hold a thought, so that you are attuned to an event or an idea, whatever the subject of your concentration may be.

Meditation is active listening to the world within by closing yourself to the thoughts of the world without. For the advancing student of the Tree of Life, regular meditation is as vital as breathing. It produces a state of consciousness in which only the metaphysical point of view is important. In its dynamic waiting-and-watching, meditation can be as exciting and joyous as it always was for the great yogi Sri Ramakrishna. In the Christian sense, it is often described as a form of silent prayer.

As mentioned in Chapter 7, *Contemplation is an elevated state of alert and conscious observation.* It is difficult to define because it is on a level where words are limiting. In Far-Eastern thought, contemplation is an *impersonal one-pointedness* of thought upon a given subject or object. And yet it opens the gates to awareness of the essence of things, and is a completely *personal* experience. Contemplation is often the beautiful result of deep meditation.

Returning to the two ways of meditation, let us first look at:

I. *Meditation concerning events of daily life.*

Use outer events to uncover your inner life. Everyday problems are your best teachers. Use notebook to jot down your daily thoughts for reviewing later.

1. In your meditation, trace outer events as far back as memory will allow. Start with the last event in the evening and go back to the first event in the morning, then yesterday, last week, last month and further back to last year, and on, until you reach the first cause of today's last event. Let these thoughts and feelings filter through your consciousness.

2. Establish the habit of examining your inner realizations in the same manner.

3. Immediately after meditation, make notes. Keep a record of your reactions. Jot them down in your notebook, or tape record your thoughts concerning the happenings of the day.

4. What are your intuitive and emotional responses to the day's events? Are they positive or negative? Add them to your notes.

5. At the end of a month, listen carefully to yourself through your accumulated notes or tapes. This period of self-analysis will help you discover yourself. If you are using your handwritten notes, they will refresh your memory and bring realization which, otherwise, may have been forgotten.

6. Later, when well versed with the Tree branches, you may incorporate this meditation in your Tree meditation by projecting the day's events on the respective Tree branches.

II. *Meditation on the Tree of Life*

1. If the Tree of Life is still new to you, have a Tree of Life diagram in front of you and, with a pencil or pen, draw the path of the Lightning Flash between the branches using strong strokes.

2. Once familiar with the Tree, close your eyes, and visualize the ten branches. Then observe how the Lightning Flash zigzags down from the Great Beyond, and emanates the ten "globes" on its way.

3. Starting at the top, and with your eyes closed, plunge mentally into each Tree branch from One to Ten. Identify with its qualities, compare the characteristics of each branch with the qualities within you. Envision each branch clearly. Cling to it so that it does not drift away; if it does, bring the picture back, gently. Do not push.

4. Each branch is equally important, but you may, as many do, discover a personal aversion to one or the other. Such a Tree branch then requires your special attention in meditation and study. In time you will find the reason for your aversion, and resistance usually evaporates.

5. If you do not have enough time to go through all Tree branches in each meditation, go back to your stopping point on the next; but always start with the path of the Lightning Flash, and with a quick review of previous branches.

6. When your meditation terminates, jot down your reactions to the individual branches.

7. Repeat these meditations until you know your personal relationship to the ten Tree branches.

8. Then you can start to contemplate the relationships between the Tree branches, but be sure to consider the exact position of each branch on the Tree of Life. For instance: branch Number Three is in opposition to branch Number Two; it dwells in the World of Creation, is part of the Supernal Triangle, and it heads the reflective-receptive-preserving Pillar of Severity.

9. In meditating on the twenty-two paths, follow

the Lightning Flash in reverse. Start at the bottom of the Tree and travel the paths to the top. In other words, start with path thirty-two and go up the Tree to path eleven.

What the wormlike cater-pillar believes to be his end, the beautiful butter-fly knows is only the be-ginning of its life.

15
Travels through Seven Planes

Natural divisions of the Tree of Life make it clear that each of us in reality has five interpenetrating bodies wrapped in one skin. We are *threefold* in essence and fabric (spirit, soul and physical body); *fourfold* in alchemical makeup; *tenfold* in traditional constitution (the branches of the Tree of Life); *twelvefold* in the measures of space and time; and *sevenfold* in metaphysical existence. We are reminded that, according to Pythagoras, the Number Seven signifies spiritual transformation in balanced cyclic evolution.

The sevenfold horizontal division of the Tree introduces definite levels of universal awareness. Moreover, it illustrates the presence of two vital forces. One is descending and creating, the other ascending and evolving, for there is a continuous downward (contracting) movement and, at the same time, a continuous upward (expanding) movement through the seven planes. The downward travel is in "being," the upward travel in "becoming." Each

Figure 35. The Seven Planes of Existence

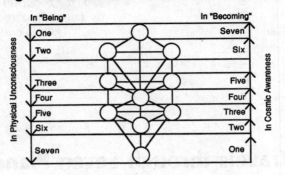

plane is of two different natures, depending on its universal number (Figure 35).

On the way down the Tree of Life (numbered from One to Seven), the seven planes illustrate creation. They represent the materialization of Adam Kadmon, the perfect cosmic human, in the *state of being*. The descending steps, though not in our scope of awareness, are compressing. They lead from pure light to pulsating life, from the subtlest to the coarsest, from the sublime to the physical, and from the cause to the effect.

On the way up the Tree of Life, the seven planes do not change as such, but their number (from One to Seven) reverses direction. Then the seven planes represent evolution in the *state of becoming*, that is the spiritualization of matter and of humanity. The ascending steps—now in cosmic awareness—are expanding and liberating. They lead from earthly life to transcendent light, from the coarsest to the subtlest, from the plight of day-to-day struggle to freedom, and from the last effect back to the first cause.

It is again by way of the qualities of numbers that the Tree of Life can illustrate the metaphysical evolution and transformation of universe and humankind.

A meditation on Figure 28 will help your understanding and memory.

Starting on the top of the Tree of Life, we are in the World of Origination, in the first plane of being. It is the divine world and the realm of the Godhead. In the second plane, we are in the Creative World of Wisdom and Understanding. It is the world of archetypes, the realm of great mystery where cherubim and seraphim sing hallelujahs in unison. In the third plane, we are in the World of Formation, in the abundance and restriction of limitless forces. It is the realm of compassion and discipline, the governing powers in the moral world. In the fourth plane and midway in involution, we are in the heart of the Tree, and in the abode of Beauty the King where love, harmony and beauty reign. It is the realm of cosmic consciousness, the plane of sacrifice and transformation, and the turning point where divinity is human and where humanity becomes divine. In the fifth plane, we are in the Worlds of Victory and Glory in Splendor, the emotional and mental planes of existence. It is the realm where functioning thoughts and feelings meet and merge. In the sixth plane, we are in the Foundation, the densest part of the formative world, and we move—in psychic consciousness— with the ebb and flow of time. We experience the battle of the sexes, and have the urgent desire to act. This is the realm where the astral and etheric bodies join. Lastly, in the seventh plane we are in the Kingdom, in the World of Action and under the magnetic pull of planet Earth. Here, in the physical world of the Four Elements of Life, all upward ways start again and again. We experience motion, sensation and duality in *all* manifestation. With a somewhat petrified brain consciousness we are neither *really* aware of our noble heritage, nor of the unity between cause and effect. Only a faint memory of that reality comes forth as a yearning for freedom on higher grounds and for a home in "the Father's many mansions." This then, is the turning point and the seventh state of being becomes the first state of becoming.

Beginning at the bottom of the Tree of Life, the first plane is now in the Kingdom, the second in the Foundation, the third in the World of Victory and Glory in Splendor. In the fourth plane (the heart of the Tree) we are again midway in evolution, and in the abode of Beauty the King. The fifth plane in ascent is the governing World of Formation, with all its abundance and restriction. In the sixth plane we are in the creative World of Wisdom and Understanding. And finally, in the seventh plane, we merge with the Godhead.

Until now we have always followed the creative downward flow of light. The reason has been to make us aware of the strong downward sweep of the universal Lightning Flash. But the redeeming upward forces are always there, even though they are constantly counteracted by the downward push of the Lightning Flash and the magnetic pull of our planet Earth.

My Teacher said: "In the universe energies are constantly involving and evolving. Descending involution transforms the fine into the coarse. Ascending evolution refines the coarse. In other words, in creation (the way down the Tree) we are in the mind of God. In our transformation (the way up the Tree) we are in the heart of God."

Again and again, the Tree of Life helps us realize that on our planet Earth—in the sacred space of the Kingdom—we always walk on hallowed ground. With this profound realization we awaken.

And a ladder set up on the earth and the top of it reached to heaven; and behold the angels of God ascending and descending on it.

Genesis 28:12

16
Stairways to Light: Climbing the Tree of Life

To find your way to freedom from the terrestrial twilight back to the radiant light above, the Tree of Life becomes a secure stairway and your scaffolding from mortal to transcendental awareness. It is the golden ladder which the Patriarch Jacob saw in his prophetic dream.

There are actually two ways to ascend the Tree of Life. One follows the Lightning Flash in reverse; it is the occult Path of Initiation also known as the winding Path of the Serpent. The other follows the Tree's middle Pillar of Mildness, and is the straight and narrow Path of Illumination, often called the Path of the Arrow.

Usually we are not given the memory of our descent from light into physical life, but our ascent into light must be in full cosmic awareness. Moreover, while the descent into life along the branches of the

Tree of Life is the same for all humankind and in close contact with the Creator, we are alone in our individual ascent into light. It *must* be that way since all spiritual evolvement is purely personal, according to an individual's metaphysical development and intensity of effort. Obviously, our journey into light is lonely and long, but all humankind will have to make it sooner or later.

In ancient times it was different. Then, in the mystery schools of Egypt, Persia and Greece (the wellspring from which science and philosophy emerged), both the descent and ascent of the human soul were dramatically enacted by the priesthood with ornate rituals in sacred symbols. After arduous training, every adept was initiated into the great mysteries by *actually* going through a personal metaphysical trail; first by descending from divinity into terrestrial existence, and then by observing the spiritual ascent from the utterly human to the supremely divine.[16] Today, the Tree of Life illustrates both: first the descent into life, and then the roads of ascent back into light.

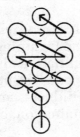

With the Tree of Life as a road map, the Path of Initiation is actually the easier of the two. Difficult though it may seem, the way to the goal is clear. It is a step-by-step journey, and goes from the last effect back to the primal cause.

To start this path, follow the practical pointers given in Chapter 14.

In your ascent, notice the perpetual downward pull of the Lightning Flash and the hold-back force of earth—magnetism. In time, you will overcome the apparent delay. Remain ever aware of your changing "environment" and of the relationship between your present Tree branch and the one you are yearning to reach.

For example: consider yourself still a resident in the Kingdom (10). Contemplate what independence and interdependence mean to you on all cosmic levels of existence. Thoughts along these lines make it easier to leave the sensory brain consciousness of earth and reach the machinery of the universe in the Foundation (9). Be aware of the approaching closeness of the swiftly changing moon and of a surrounding psychic consciousness. Try to experience the relativity of time and space on the terrestrial level. Look patiently into the eyes and the soul of people around you rather than noticing their outer appearances.

Moving from the Foundation (9) to the Glory in Splendor (8) in the abode of the planet Mercury, notice your discriminating mind's ability and speed in separating and transforming all kinds of thought. Again, observe your mind's clarity and its polar-relationship to the forthcoming stream of emotions from Victory (7) in the abode of the planet Venus. It is important to remember that, in evolution, humans felt before they could think; now you have to think before your feelings can be clarified. But always follow the impulse of your heart through the reasoning of your mind. Let neither work independently in reaching any decision. Together, mind and heart are an infallible team; independently, they are adversaries.

It takes time and practice to balance your arising thoughts with your feelings and to do so without swinging from one to the other, like a pendulum. Only after that balance is achieved can you reach out to Beauty the King (6) and experience genuine love, harmony and beauty. These moments of rest in the Tree of Life's heart will be hard to leave, but one must encounter the Martian and catabolic qualities of Severity-Justice (5) in the abode of the planet Mars. There you will meet the power of the law of cause and effect, and experience all kinds of stress. You encounter struggle, restriction and frustration, particularly with the removal of much accumulated wealth that had turned into waste. You also must strike a balance with abundance and charisma in Mercy-Abundance (4), the abode of the planet Jupiter. Again, you have to achieve and maintain the essential harmony between severity and restriction (5) as the awakened cosmic memory of abundance and true empathy (4) comes to the fore. Until the governing powers of the universe can be balanced within you, your further climb into light must come to a halt.

When, at long last, you reach the great Understanding (3) of eternal womb-man-hood in the abode of the planet Saturn (with all its pains and sorrows), you face the most difficult step. Now you have to link your infinite Understanding with infinite Wisdom (2), the eternal maleness of life. And when harmony is achieved in you between the free-moving, fertilizing powers that generate strength, and those that give form and preserve the greatness of creation, you—like Enoch—will have attained union with the light of the I Am That I Am. This is your homecoming.

How long will it take to climb the Ladder of Light one step at a time? How many weeks, months, years or aeons? You know by now that the time needed will depend on your own effort, and, of course, on your individual capacity and personal spiritual involvement. Even with eternity before all of us, why should we wait? Start now, particularly since it is possible to reach cosmic consciousness, that is the awareness of the soul's oneness with the All (Tree Branch 6) while still in your terrestrial robe of flesh. Even an occasional glimpse of that vision will give you courage and strength on the way.

The other way up the Tree of Life is the Path of Illumination. It is the Bible's straight and narrow path for the very few mystics and high initiates who have already mastered the wisdom of harmony between all pairs of opposites. This road leads from the Kingdom (10) to the Foundation (9); from there to Beauty the King (6) and through the hidden Daath on to the Godhead in the Crown (1).

This was the path of Gautama the Buddha and of Jesus the Christ, who had both already attained cosmic consciousness and whose thoughts and feelings were no longer moved by earthly ebbs and tides.

They were willing to make any sacrifice and to die for their convictions. According to the Great Plan of Life, they were compassionately at the service of humanity.

On their Path of the Arrow, these and a very few other enlightened human beings move *between* Severity-Justice (5) and Mercy-Abundance (4), and *between* Understanding (3) and Wisdom (2). They partake of both their qualities, and yet are neither. But they all have to pierce through Daath which, in their cases, seems to be the Dark Night of the Soul of which St. John of the Cross gave such vivid testimony.

Aware of the infinite power from above, and drawing constantly from its light, these illuminated human beings stand alone in the world. Yet they *know* that they never stand by themselves.

Some Final Words

Yes, you have come a long, long way. Once no more than a desire in the creative universal mind, you have journeyed from the Great Beyond along the eternal path of the Lightning Flash.

All is well. The Tree of Life has grown its branches; it is heavy with fruit. You move freely in solid matter and sense how alive you are. You know that your breath is still the very life breath of your Creator.

Deep within yourself you have touched the many dimensions of freedom. You saw how the invisible became visible. Tomorrow you may change the finite into infinity, and reach an eternity beyond all galaxies. If you but will, make every moment count. Fulfill your fondest dreams, and you help fulfill the Great Plan of Life.

In conclusion, let me share the final words of my Teacher at our last meeting. He said, "You may often stand alone in life, but you never stand by yourself. Because, just as you cannot separate from your own shadow, so are all the qualities of the Tree of Life deep within you. You are, in fact, the living Tree of Life . . . built of Fire, Water, Air and Earth . . . linked to the chain of cause and effect . . . moved by the rhythm of time in space . . . growing with contradictions and many a paradox . . . and working in dualities by oppositions. And yet nothing can ever be added to your perfection. Remove the tarnish and uncover your pure being.

"Uncover it . . . uncover it, so that, in moments of silence and tranquillity, you too will *feel* that it is the Creator who looks through *your* eyes, listens through *your* ears, and feels through *your* heart. Then, and only then, will you *know* that it is the endless chain of creation and the sacred space in You that, joyfully, co-creates, while it feels and thinks and loves and shares. For You are

Infinity's End!"

Appendix
Kabbalah: Its Myth, Tradition,
Books and Personalities

The story behind the story of the Tree of Life has the
sanctity of ages behind it. It is shrouded in mystery
and steeped in the ancient tradition of the Kabbalah
(meaning in Hebrew "received tradition"). The fact
that the root K-B-L also signifies "by mouth to ear"
indicates that Kabbalah was, at one time, a sacred
and secret unwritten book.

With the Tree of Life at its core, Kabbalah is (as
already stated) the mystical religious philosophy of
the Hebrews. Its study of the wisdom hidden in the
words of the holy Scriptures (known to the world as
the Bible's Old Testament) is especially concerned
with the opening chapters of the books of Genesis
and Ezekiel which unfold the beginning of creation.
The Kabbalah, although faithful to the ways of its
Patriarchal Fathers, is not a rigid system of knowledge but a steadily evolving doctrine of faith. Its

complex thoughts are neither totally Hebrew in concept nor unified in one single book.

Let us look at a few fragments of the engrossing background of the Tree of Life. These do not pretend to trace so manifold a tale in which—like a metaphysical detective story—much historical evidence (including the authorship of prominent books) remains hidden to this day.

It was not until almost five millennia after recorded Jewish history (the 1200s of our era) that the word "Kabbalah" was coined, seemingly in Rabbi Isaac the Blind's inner circle in southern France. Up to that time the occult teachings were referred to as Inner Wisdom, a Way of Truth or the Science of Truth. Transmitted only to a carefully selected few, those mystical seekers of truth were known as Children of Faith, Men of Belief, Fearers of Sin, Visitors from Paradise, the Understanding Ones, the Wise-Hearted, Masters of Mystery, Those Who Know Measures, Worthy Ones, Masters of Service, or simply Those Who Know.

It was around the thirteenth or fourteenth century that an arbitrary classification of the Kabbalah doctrine was started.[17] It imitated the division developed for other sacred Judaic literature by Rabbi Moses ben Maimon, who was known as Maimonides or Rambam. It is worth noting that this erudite Spanish philosopher and mathematician was also the personal physician to the great Sultan Saladin.

When, where and how the Kabbalah actually began is still a puzzle in the minds of searching scholars, but not in the hearts of faithful mystics. To them, myth and legend come much closer to reality than recorded history.

Wherever history hides, legend (which is the fiction of myth) can flourish. So it is with this primordial wisdom-tradition. Legend is heaped upon legend, each ready to tell its colorful and sometimes conflicting tale, each "divinely empowered" and mostly carried by winged messengers. One such legend is quick to tell that the Lord God Himself taught the wisdom to His self-chosen company of angels in paradise. Another myth gives a different line of transmission: the Lord God revealed its secrets to Melchizedek, the priest-king of Salem who, in turn, initiated Abraham, the nomad Patriarch and "friend of God." According to yet another legend, the Kabbalah came to Adam and Eve through angels directed by the Lord God. And another myth seems certain that Daniel brought the mystical truth from Chaldea to his people in Palestine.

In his book *Qabalah*, Isaac Myer reports, what some Kabbalists claim, that the sacred wisdom may have gone from Adam to Seth, from Seth to Noah, and on to Abraham, who in the Land of the Nile, taught carefully selected parts to a very few Egyptians worthy of this privilege. Among them was Moses (an Egyptian initiate), who continued its studies during his forty years in the Sinai. Eventually Moses (by then a great prophet) shared the oral teachings with his Seventy Elders and also with the sons of Jacob, the future Twelve Tribes of Israel. As time moved on, this strong chain of initiation touched the prophets Isaiah, Ezekiel and Daniel. It reached King David and the wise Solomon, as the biblical Psalms, Proverbs and the Song of Solomon vividly testify.

"It came from the night of time and a land now lost," another legend asserts. And it may well be that the high priests of Atlantis and Egypt, and later the Chaldean magi, knew of the sacred wisdom long before the Hebrew people became the custodians of this precious legacy.

Where does legend end and history begin? Seemingly, Kabbalah was an oral teaching tradition for a long, long time. Some of its secrets were given in numerical symbols instead of words. To avoid misuse and distortion, this "unwritten book" was moved cautiously in an unbroken chain from the teacher's lips into the ears of "even-keeled men of good character who practiced good deeds." Among them were the pietist Hasidim of old, a few learned Pharisees, and—as the Dead Sea Scrolls indisputably testify—the ascetic Essenes, who studied and practiced the Sacred Truth in their communal life. Yeshua ben Miriam, the Rabbi of Galilee, better known to the world as Jesus Christ, is revered by many as a very special Kabbalist initiate. His teaching of the Beatitudes and the Lord's Prayer (Matthew 5:3-12 and 6:9-13) speak louder than unrecorded history.

As can be seen from this historical overview, Kabbalistic wisdom changed meaning and direction with every change in the dramatic life of the Jews. While it unfolded in time and space, the same golden thread of the cherished and sacred tradition was always woven into its fabric. Yet the teachings became increasingly abstract and complex, and today's "total Kabbalah" can only be for those well anchored in the observance and ceremony of traditional Judaism. Even then, serious study and practice demand a competent teacher's guidance and supervision. The reason is simple. The powerful transfer of spiritual knowledge *must* be fitted to the student's metaphysical capacity and go hand in hand with essential verbal explanations.

Today, "Kabbalah" is a collective term which embraces practically every school of Jewish mysticism and blends the mystery of the universe with our divine heritage.

In days long gone by, the mystical wisdom was the aristocratic privilege of a select few, the shadow of which remains today in a sizable body of allegories. Later on, the Kabbalah incorporated rabbinical, moral and even legal views, as they were deemed necessary.

From about 100 B.C. (or B.C.E., meaning before the common era, as Jews prefer to call the period B.C.) for roughly a thousand years, the esoteric tradition was known as "Merkabah mysticism." It was a mysticism of ecstasy, and was mainly concerned with the story of creation according to the prophet Ezekiel's vision of the fourfold throne chariot (the *Merkabah*), as recorded in the Book of Ezekiel. Between the fifth and the sixth centuries A.D., the *Heikhalot Books* highlighted the seven heavenly palaces or halls (*heikhalot*) through which man's soul must pass on the way to the Merkabah. Many existing Merkabah writings remain unpublished to this day.

In the 1200s the term "Kabbalah" signified "Medieval Jewish Mysticism" and the Merkabah doctrine started to fade into the background. Some hundred years later, the *Zohar* made its dramatic appearance in Spain, and the Golden Age of the Kabbalah had dawned. While history and accuracy remained traditionally inseparable, the formerly sacred teachings gained steadily in popularity and interest, particularly among certain non-Hebrew scholars, mystics and theologians.

In time, the Kabbalah continued to reach further ground. It became generally accepted as being based on both the spoken and the written word: (1) the Oral Law given to Moses on the Sinai, along with (2) the Written Law in the Old Testament's first five books, the Torah (meaning "guidance"). Then, in the middle 1500s, a new "Lurianic Kabbalah" blossomed in the Community of the Devout, the center school of Safed in Upper Galilee. And in the middle 1700s (c. 1698-1760) the latest phase of Jewish mysticism, called the modern Hasidic movement, appeared in Poland and Russia by way of Germany. Founded by Israel ben Eliezer, known as the Baal Shem Tov (the Master of the Good Name), this mystical path embraces human self-knowledge and greater closeness to the Creator through Torah study and community living. In order to hasten the coming of the Messiah, its living doctrine includes exalted communal and solitary prayers, contemplation and meditation. For many experts and devotees, Martin Buber ranks as its outstanding twentieth-century exponent.

Kabbalistic literature is extensive and steadily on the increase. According to one count there are today over 3,000 printed books and papers, and about three times as many unpublished manuscripts waiting for the printer's ink. During the last two decades popular books on the "Kabbalah" have mushroomed.

Among mountains of Kabbalistic literature (and mostly for studious reading), the following three books are of special interest to students of the Tree of Life:

First is the oldest document on the subject, and the first written in Hebrew: *The Book of Formation*, often called the *Book of Creation* (*Sepher Yetzirah* in Hebrew). Dressed in symbols and compressed into fewer than 2,000 words, the book's six short chapters make laconic, sometimes oracular statements with no further explanation. Seemingly, this slim book is a visionary experience concerning the creative elements of the universe—a fundamental commentary on a cosmogony and cosmology, if you will, in which numbers, letters and sounds are the tools of creation and the foundation of all things.

Over the years, the book has been translated into several languages, and the clarity of the text may have suffered occasionally. Several English editions include a later supplement, the *Thirty-Two Paths of Wisdom*, which refers to *The Book of Formation's* opening sentence, and the thirty-two mysterious paths of wisdom through which God created his universe.

Some scholars believe that this mysterious treatise is a fragment. In actual circulation since the thirteenth century, scholars date the writing of the book anywhere from 2000 B.C. to 600 A.D. There are conflicting views about its authors. Some consider it the revelation of the Patriarch Abraham (about 2000 B.C.). Others ascribe it to the erudite Rabbi Akiva ben Joseph (between 50 and 135 A.D.). Again, to mystical seekers after truth, the actual date is not all-important.

The next book of special interest is the *Book Bahir*, sometimes called simply *Bahir* (*Sepher ha-Bahir* in

Hebrew), also known as the *Book of Brilliance*. Labeled by many as the oldest theology in gnostic tradition, this small book of about 12,000 words is written in a mixture of Hebrew and Aramaic. It appeared at the end of the twelfth century in southern France, and its authorship is still uncertain. Some modern historians attribute the book to the French Rabbi Isaac the Blind, lovingly known as the Father of the Kabbalah. He originated the names of the ten branches of the Tree of Life, which remain unchanged to this day. Possibly though, Azriel ben Menachem of Gerona (about 1160 to 1238 A.D.), the leading disciple of Isaac the Blind, was the author of the *Bahir*. Or it could be that Rabbi Azriel took the name of the Spanish talmudist Rabbi Nachmanides (Moses ben Nachman), since the pseudepigraphic form of authorship was often used in the Middle Ages, especially in Jewish circles.

The *Bahir* introduced the concept of the *Shekhinah* (the "Divine Presence") as the feminine attribute and Heavenly Mother at the side of the patriarchal God the Father.

At about the time the *Bahir* appeared, the *Commentary on the Ten Sephiroth* was published in question-and-answer form, and was attributed at a later date to Rabbi Azriel ben Menachem. Along with the *Bahir* and the *Heikhalot Books*, this commentary was a prominent source for Kabbalistic study until, less than a century later, the *Zohar* emerged.

The third book of interest, the *Zohar*, also known as the *Book of Splendor* (*Sepher ha-Zohar* in Hebrew), is the classic, canonical text of the Kabbalah.

Often considered a mystical commentary on passages of the Torah, it concerns itself with the transition from the infinite to the finite, and with the inner meaning of the law in the Hebrew scriptures.

The *Zohar* made its appearance in Spain in the late 1300s. Written in Aramaic and Hebrew, this awesome work of nineteen parts and some 2,500 pages has been translated into many languages and reprinted in numerous editions. The renowned Dr. Gershom G. Scholem said: "The *Zohar* is written . . . almost, one might say, in the form of a mystical novel." He adds, "It is a mixture of theosophic theology, mythical cosmogony, mystical psychology and anthropology," and "one of the most remarkable works of Jewish literature and of the literature of mysticism in general."

Trying to trace the origin and authorship of the *Zohar* still comes as close to academic crystal-ball gazing as it did some 600 years ago. Was it the work of Rabbi Simeon ben Yohai, revered as the Holy Lamp of Israel and the illustrious disciple of the great Rabbi and mystic Akiva ben Joseph? When condemned to death by the Roman Emperor Hadrian at the time of the cruel destruction of the second Temple of Jerusalem, Rabbi Simeon escaped imprisonment and, together with his son Eleazer, hid in a cave for thirteen years. There, while contemplating the divine mysteries of the Torah, he was frequently visited by the prophet Elijah, so legend tells. After his father's death, Rabbi Eleazer collected the oral revelations in a book which was supposedly found in a cave near Galilee in the 1300s. Was it or was it not the *Zohar*?

Or was it the penmanship of Rabbi Moses de Leon,

who published the *Zohar* under the by-line of Rabbi Simeon ben Yohai in the Spanish town of Gerona during the late 1300s? Today some experts consider Rabbi Moses the father of the *Zohar* while others believe it to be Rabbi Simeon.

Be that as it may, the *Zohar* reached an ever-widening public in the century to follow. When the Jews were expelled from Spain in 1492, the *Zohar*—like Christopher Columbus—left the "old home" in search of a new and better one. It traveled with the exiles to France, Italy and Palestine. From there it moved farther into Morocco, Turkey, Poland and Germany. Everywhere the *Zohar* met with genuine interest. It exerted a marked influence on both Christendom and Islam, and thus spread its roots deep in the world at large.

Of illustrious Kabbalists in the 1500s, three scholarly mystics elevated the Kabbalah to an all-time peak. It was at the Community of the Devout in Safed that the Spanish Rabbi Moses Cordovero (1522-1570), a systematic theologian and prolific writer, gave a new twist to Kabbalistic thinking. At about the same time, Rabbi Isaac Luria, born to a German family in Jerusalem and a one-time pupil of Cordovero, presented his novel mystical and visionary views. Called "the Ari" (meaning "lion" in Hebrew), the wonder-working Rabbi had found the *Zohar* and studied the Kabbalah in Cairo, Egypt. During his three-year stay in Safed, he became the leading figure of a new Lurianic Kabbalah. To this day, the Ari is considered *the* authority on later, modern Kabbalism.

Luria did little writing during his all-too-short life (1534-1572). But his foremost disciple, Rabbi

Hayyim Vital (Calabrese) (1543-1620), devoted more than twenty years to assembling Luria's notes, and later authored his master's teachings, which included a volume called *The Tree of Life*. Soon thereafter, Luria's Kabbalistic thoughts were incorporated into the liturgy as well as into Jewish home life and became part of the mystical theology of Judaism.

A word about prominent non-Hebrew Kabbalists. From 1200 or so onward, more and more Christian and Muslim scholars became interested in Kabbalistic wisdom, and parallel movements started here and there, particularly in middle Europe and England.

Among the many, you will find such eminent names as Meister Eckhart, the German theologian; Raymond Lully, the Catalonian chemist and metaphysician; Johannes Reuchlin, the renowned scholar of Oriental literature; Pico della Mirandola, a famous philosopher; Paul Ricius, the personal physician of Emperor Maximilian of the Holy Roman Empire; the occult philosopher and physician Cornelius H. Agrippa of Nettelsheim; Cardinal E. de Viterbo; the Franciscan Francesco Giorgio of Venice; the Frenchman Guillaume Postel, the first to translate *The Book of Formation* and the *Zohar* into Latin; the "Philosophus Teutonicus" cobbler, Jakob Boehme of Görlitz; the famous mystic William Blake; and Christian Knorr von Rosenroth, who translated parts of the *Zohar* into Latin.

In the late 1800s a lively interest in Kabbalistic teachings expressed itself in such metaphysical organizations as the Hermetic Order of the Golden Dawn, the Society of Inner Light, some esoteric groups of

Rosicrucians, and the Theosophical Society. The latter's founder, the Russian noblewoman Helena Petrovna Blavatsky (1831-1891), herself a learned Kabbalist, inspired several of her students to delve into productive Kabbalistic studies. The books of William Wynn Westcott, Eliphas Levi, Papus (Encossé), and G. R. S. Mead are only a part of that roster. More recently, Dr. Carl G. Jung (1875-1961) is said to have based the archetype principle of his analytical psychology on the Tree of Life.

Other prominent non-Hebrew Kabbalist mystics who lived during the past eight centuries include Pope Sixtus IV, Pietro de Albano, Copernicus, Dante, Dr. John Dee, Robert Fludd, Fabre d'Olivet, Jesuit Athanasius Kircher, G. Leibnitz, Sir Isaac Newton and Benjamin Franklin.

Within the last hundred years popular books on Kabbalah in general and on the Tree of Life in particular have been on the increase. They have literally mushroomed in recent decades. Some of the authors are Aleister Crowley, Perle Epstein, Dion Fortune, Adolphe Franck, J. F. C. Fuller, Christian D. Ginsburg, William G. Gray, Z'ev ben Shimon Halevi, Dr. Anna Kingsford, Gareth Knight, Jeff Love, MacGregor Mathers, Isaac Myer, Charles Poncé, Israel Regardie, Edouard Schuré, Carlo Suarés, A. E. Waite and William Wynn Westcott. Four twentieth-century Jewish scholars wrote books for laymen: Rabbi Aryeh Kaplan, Rabbi Levi I. Krakovsky, Rabbi Zalman Schachter and Rabbi Herbert Weiner.

And all the while, the golden thread of the ancient Kabbalistic tradition continues to be woven into the fabric of Hebrew life. Today, earnest endeavors are under way to rebuild Luria's famous Kabbalah Center in Safed, and there is also an International Center for Kabbalah Research at the Hebrew University in Jerusalem. According to expert opinion, the "scholarly investigation of the Kabbalah is only now emerging from its infancy." And in true Jewish tradition this "infancy" is almost 6,000 years old, give or take a few Hebrew calendar years and lunar months.

Yes, tradition is a treasure. And it always remembers . . . as it is told in Genesis 3:24:

"To keep the way of the Tree of Life!"

Notes

¹Hermes Trismegistus is the legendary Egyptian priest-philosopher-king of supreme wisdom who authored some 20,000 sacred books and was hailed as Master of Masters and Scribe of the Gods. Some scholars believe that this "thrice-great" mythical personage existed before the times of Moses, between the 15th and 13th century B.C. The eternal Law of Correspondence, "as above so below; as below so above," is attributed to him, and was engraved in the eighth-century Emerald Tablets.

²Perennial Wisdom is frequently referred to as Science of the Soul, Divine Knowledge or Ageless Wisdom. It is said to be as old as time, and embodies that primordial truth which is the mystical core and essence of all true religions and philosophies. It illustrates the Laws of Life in their harmonious interrelationships.

In times long past, perennial wisdom was consid-

ered sublime Wisdom Religion. Later, and for fear of
dangerous misuse by the profane, its sacred teachings were hidden. Only learned adepts transmitted
the wisdom orally to a very few prudently selected
students.

Recently the Perennial Wisdom has come to the
fore again. Cloaked in contemporary language, its
unchanging truth flourishes amid neon lights, com-
puters, and man-made satellites. Now it is here to
stay. Its eternally fresh message ends the illusion of
separateness and is open to all in search of a meaningful life. It is occult only to the extent that it is not
understood.

[3]Derived from the Greek, the word "symbol"
means "a sign." A symbol is a lively thought form, a
figurative shorthand or picture language to describe
something other than itself in a manner that everyday words could not achieve. Moreover, symbols can
express that which in itself is expressionless. By being plain and direct, symbols reach every heart and
mind on one's individual personal level of conscious
understanding. To a simple person, the symbol is
simple; to a sophisticated person, the symbol is complex. This is why sacred scriptures, parables, fairy
tales and fables use the simple language of symbols
to tell of that lofty reality which is beyond manifestation. In that sense, symbols are the physical repre-
sentation of inner qualities, and the language to link
life's many dimensions.

It has been said that absolute truth can only be
touched through symbols. That means that a truth
which can be put into words can never be the total
truth.

According to the renowned psychologist, Carl G.

Jung, symbols touch the human conscious and unconscious simultaneously. Like music they dissolve
language barriers, and they unite people when words
would divide or separate. To the Roman Catholic
monk Thomas Merton, in contrast, a true symbol is
an object pointing to a subject.

Symbols call attention to the real rather than to the
apparent or to the relative.

From a holistic viewpoint there are two types of
symbols: natural symbols, which in themselves represent a reality, such as sunshine signifying light
and life, or winter meaning cold and dark; and man-
made symbols, which through continued use reveal
a reality, such as the use of alphabet letters for reading and writing. Modern people cannot be without
the use of symbols to project the real. Flags or banners to represent their nations are just one example.
Among the many symbols that mark our daily rou-
tine are postal stamps, watches, calendars, comput-
ers and checkbooks.

[4]Cosmic Trees are symbolic trees of unknown origin. They rank among the very oldest images known.
As thought-forms, they express our natural longing
for a link with the heavens, between the seen and the
unseen.

Perhaps the original thought behind the symbol
was that of a natural tree with its rhythmic seasonal
transformation from barrenness to blossoms, leaves
and fruits. The tree illustrated eternal life in its four
stages: divine origin, transcendental beginning, continuous renewal and perpetual growth.

In the cosmology of sacred scriptures, the Tree of
Life always occupies a central place as a representative form of creation. Often called the Tree of Heav-

en, the World Tree and the Body of God, it is also referred to as the Tree of Perfection, the Tree of Immortality or simply the Sacred Tree.

In the first pages of the Old Testament, we find the Tree of Life in the paradise of the unawakened man. Again, on the last page of the New Testament, in the New Jerusalem, it is the home of the enlightened one. The Tree in paradise presents its sustaining quality and promises the continuity of life. In the New Jerusalem, the Tree tells of twelve manners of fruit (symbolic of the zodiac), and reveals its leaves to be the healing life force of humankind.

The respective Biblical passages are:

Genesis 2:9: "And out of the ground made the Lord God to grow every tree that is pleasant to the sight, and good for food; the tree of life also in the midst of the garden, and the tree of knowledge of good and evil."

Genesis 3:22: "And the Lord God said, Behold, the man has become as one of us, to know good and evil; and now, lest he put forth his hand and take also of the tree of life, and eat, and live forever."

Genesis 3:24: "So he drove out the man; and he placed at the east of the garden of Eden Cherubims, and a flaming sword which turned every way, to keep the way of the tree of life."

Revelation 22:2: "In the midst of the street of it, and on either side of the river, was there the tree of life, which bare twelve manner of fruits, and yielded her fruit every month; and the leaves of the fruit were for the healing of all nations."

Revelation 22:14: " . . . that they may have the right to the tree of life, and may enter through the gates into the city."

In the Maitreya Upanishads, the *lingam*, a World Tree, symbolizes the legendary Hindu trinity as the "threefold Brahman with its roots above," namely: Brahma, the creator; Vishnu, the preserver; and Shiva, the dissolver and restorer. The Rig Vedas and Upanishads mention the very same tree as Brahman-rooted which, from one single root above, spreads throughout the entire universe.

In the *Bhagavad Gita*, Chapter 15, Lord Krishna speaks of "a fig tree in ancient story, the giant Asvattha, the everlasting; rooted in heaven, its branches earthward; each of the leaves is a song of the Vedas; and he who knows it, knows all the Vedas."

The *Katha Upanishad* tells of the divine origin: "This eternal Asvattha whose roots rise high and whose branches grow low is the pure, the Brahman."

According to legend, Lord Krishna was conceived by the saintly Devaki while she was sleeping under the wide, shady branches of a tree of unknown age— "a tree which the holy Rishis called The Tree of Life." And it is said that the sacred bodhi tree under which Lord Buddha attained illumination was the World Tree of Life.

In Teutonic mythology, the Scandinavian *Edda* lets the seeress Volva describe the cosmic ash tree, named Yggdrasil, as the symbol of the universe, "that tree set up in wisdom (with three great roots) which grows to the bosom of the earth. With water white is the great tree wet."

The great God Odin's spear, named Gungnir, was cut from branches of the Tree of Life.

[5]*Branches and Paths.* All told, the Tree of Life has ten branches and twenty-two connecting paths. Together, and according to *The Book of Formation*, they constitute the "thirty-two Mysterious Paths of Wisdom" with which the Creator created the universe.

The Tree branches, numbered from one to ten, are the objective building blocks of both the universe (the macrocosm) and the human (the microcosm). In connection with the thirty-two Mysterious Paths of Wisdom, the ten Tree branches count also as the first ten wisdom paths.

The twenty-two paths that connect the Tree branches are two-way channels of communication and subjective states of cosmic consciousness. The nature of each path is determined by the Tree branches it connects, and it reveals the effect of creation and also its message. Numbered from eleven to thirty-two, the paths on the Tree of Life represent primarily the twenty-two letters of the Hebrew alphabet.

[6]*Numbers in the Metaphysical Tradition* are living principles, not chosen quantities and measures. Their importance and meaning surpass the role of mathematical digits in modern everyday use.

[7]*Pairs of Opposites.* On the Tree of Life these tend to attract, resist and complement one another. They have the twofold purpose to divide and separate, in order to join and unite. And in so doing they actually bring about action, harmony and progress.

[8]According to Kabbalistic myth, the pelican is the metaphor of supreme sacrifice, and of the Hebrew letter Vav. Unable to collect food, the bird pierces her breast, and feeds her baby chicks with her own blood. In the Alchemical tradition, the pelican symbolizes the exaltation of the quintessence.

[9]Pythagoras (about 582 to 500 B.C.), the great Greek philosopher, father of mathematics and prize winner at the Olympic Games, saw the manifest world as a concordant arrangement of numbers. The mystical decad, the metaphysical quantity and quality of each number from one to ten, was the quintessence of his teachings. By illustrating the universe in unity, it was the transcendental meeting place of religion, science and art. At the Greek community college in Croton, which Pythagoras founded and headed for nearly forty years, the science of numbers (including music and arithmetic) was the required year-long training for all neophytes. A hundred years later in Plato's academy, the science of numbers was the basis of an intensive preparatory study for initiation into the ancient mysteries. Pythagoras, the "Trainer of Souls," and his ideal community exerted not only a marked influence on the ancient world of Greece, but has endured to this day.

[10]The Four Noble Truths of Buddhism are: the truth of suffering, the cause of suffering, the cessation of suffering, and the way that leads to the cessation of suffering. The way is the eightfold path, namely: right view, right intention, right speech, right action, right livelihood, right effort, right mindfulness, and right concentration.

[11]Although contemplation and meditation are not the same thing, most dictionaries draw no distinction between the two, probably because both are based on silent concentration. Both activities start in the same way, namely (1) by patiently detaching the restless mind from all immediate thoughts and things, so as to render it serene, alert, pliable and

objective; and then (2) by focusing the one-pointed mind, without any prejudice, on a chosen single object.

After these preliminary steps, meditation will bring a continuous and intense flow of clear thoughts around the object of concentration in its narrowed viewing range. The result will be an impersonal and deeper metaphysical awareness.

Contemplation, even though a different kind of concentration, is more difficult to describe in words. According to my Teacher it comes close to Zen meditation. By way of introspection and conscious receptivity, contemplation observes the chosen subject. The purpose of contemplation is expansion; it is to lose oneself in order to find oneself in an altered state of consciousness, which is the eternal now. Or, as Walt Whitman put it in his *Leaves of Grass*, it happens when one ceases to exist and starts to be.

[12]Dionysius the Areopagite is apparently the assumed name of a sixth-century Christian mystic, the legendary author of what became known as the *Dionysian angelic hierarchy*. He was probably a pupil of Proclus, the Greek writer and philosopher (c. 412-485 A.D.), who was himself one of the last of the Platonic school. Some of the Dionysian teachings are laid down in *The Mystical Theology* and *The Divine Name*. It seems quite certain that Dionysius was not the convert of Paul, the Apostle (and the first Bishop of Rome), mentioned in Acts 17:34 of the Bible.

[13]Ten Angelic Appearances are mentioned in the Bible in connection with the event of Jesus Christ. Three of these occurred before the birth of Jesus, to:

Zacharias in Luke 1:1; Mary in Luke 1:26; Joseph in Matthew 1:20.

Seven appearances manifested during the early life of Jesus, to: the shepherds in Luke 2:9; Joseph in Matthew 2:13; Joseph in Matthew 2:19; after the temptation in Matthew 4:11; in Gethsemane in Luke 22:43; at the resurrection in Matthew 28:2; at the ascension in Acts 1:10.

[14]The number thirty-two is highly significant on a metaphysical level. In the Old Testament's Five Books of Moses, thirty-two is the sum total of the first and last Hebrew letters: the number value of its first letter Beth is two and that of its last letter Lamed is thirty.

Mathematically expressed, the number thirty-two is the fifth power of the number two: $2 \times 2 \times 2 \times 2 \times 2$.

[15]The number twenty-two, in Kabbalistic tradition, symbolizes the Teacher. For example, the Hebrew alphabet has 22 letters, which are the foundation of all creation. The New Testament's Revelation has 22 chapters, which present the foundation of all *new* things. The Old Testament counts three times 22 books. According to an old Egyptian myth there are 22 keys to the secrets of nature.

The 22 Major Arcana of the Egyptian Tarot deck are another example of the Teacher. Originally, this card game was based on a sacred path of initiation ascribed to Hermes Trismegistus, as the *Book of Thoth*. When the high priests foresaw the downfall of Egypt, they cut the book into a 78-card game of 22 major and 56 minor arcana. So that its primordial wisdom might travel and teach around the globe, they put these cards into the hands of wandering gypsies.

In yet a different culture and at a different time, 22,000 workers built the Taj Mahal in 22 years.

[16]Those interested in the symbolic rituals of initiations in the Egyptian Temple of Osiris, and of the Greek mystery plays in Delphi and Eleusis, will find them vividly described in two books by Edouard Schuré, *The Great Initiates*, (St. George Books, West Nyack, New York, 1961) and *From Sphinx to Christ*, (Rudolf Steiner Publications, Blauvelt, New York, 1970).

[17]Around the thirteenth or fourteenth century Kabbalists started to make their own distinctions between parts of the total doctrine, by imitating Rabbi Maimonides' systematization of sacred Judaic literature. Among them are the following:

The unwritten Kabbalah involves the metaphysical interpretation of the truth hidden and embedded in the esoteric teachings and their practices. It is not entrusted to the uninitiated.

The mystical Kabbalah, sometimes called "speculative," illustrates the mystical nature of the Creator, of his universe and of humankind.

The dogmatic Kabbalah delves into the scholastic literature of the principal doctrines. These include the cosmogony and nature of the Creator; the cosmology of the universe and its destiny; the nature of the human soul; angels and demons; the transcendental nature of the Hebrew alphabet and of numbers; the nature of good and evil; and the balancing of opposing forces.

The practical Kabbalah, sometimes called "occult," focuses on talismanic magic and chiromancy. The use of the twenty-two Hebrew letter glyphs in their numerical values became the basis of medieval magic. It was this perception of the magical interaction of letters and numbers which, erroneously, gave the *total* Kabbalah the widespread reputation of being dangerous.

Selected Bibliography

General

The Holy Bible. Authorized King James version. New York: The New York Bible Society, n.d.

Cruden, Alexander, A.M. *Cruden's Complete Concordance to the Old and New Testaments*. Grand Rapids, MI: Zondervan Publishing Co., 1968.

The Holy Qu'an. Translated by Maulana Muhammad Ali. Chicago: Specialty Promotions Co., Inc., 1973.

The Bhagavad Gita. Translated by Swami Nikhilananda. New York: Ramakrishna-Vivekananda Center, 1952.

Bhagavad Gita, The Song of God. Translated by Swami Prabhavananda and Christopher Isherwood. Hollywood: Marcel Rudd, Co., 1944.

Akiba ben Joseph. *The Book of Formation (Sepher Yetzirah)*. Translated by Knut Stenring. New York: Ktav Publishing House, Inc., 1970.

Kalisch, Rev. Dr. Isidor. *Sepher Yezirah: A Book on Creation*. New York: L. H. Frank and Co., 1972.

Suarès, Carlo. *The Qabala Trilogy*. Boston and London: Shambhala, 1985.

Plato. *The Timaeus and the Critias*. New York: Pantheon Books, 1944.

Taylor, Bayard. *Goethe's Faust*. Boston: Houghton, Mifflin & Co., 1898.

Dictionaries

Davidson, Gustav. *A Dictionary of Angels.* New York: Free Press, 1967.

Zimmerman, J.E. *Dictionary of Classical Mythology.* New York: Bantam Books, 1966.

Further Reading

Achad, Frater. *The Anatomy of the Body of God.* New York: Samuel Weiser Inc., 1972.

_____. *The Egyptian Revival.* New York: Samuel Weiser Inc., 1969.

_____. *Q.B.L. or The Bride's Reception.* New York: Samuel Weiser Inc., 1974.

Albertson, Edward. *Understanding the Kabbalah.* Los Angeles: Sherbourne Press, Inc., 1973.

Alder, Vera Stanley. *The Finding of the Third Eye.* London: Rider and Co., 1970.

Ashlag, Rabbi Yehuda. *Kabbalah: Ten Luminous Emanations.* Jerusalem: The Press of the Research Centre of Kabbalah, 1972.

Aurobindo, Sri. *On Yoga I: The Synthesis of Yoga.* Pondicherry, India: Aurobindo Ashram Press, 1965.

_____ *A Glossary of Sanskrit Terms in the Synthesis of Yoga.* Pondicherry, India: Aurobindo Ashram Press, 1969.

Avalon, Arthur (Sir John Woodroffe). *The Serpent Power.* New York: Dover Publications, 1974.

Bennett, J.G. *The Enneagram.* Sherbourne: Coombe Spring Press, 1974.

Berg, Dr. Philip S. *Kabbalah for the Layman.* The Old City Jerusalem, Israel: Press of the Research Center of Kabbalah, 1984.

Birnbaum, Philip, trans. *Ethics of the Fathers*. New York: Hebrew Publishing Co., 1949.

Buber, Martin. *Good and Evil*. New York: Scribner's, 1952.

Bucke, Richard Maurice, M.D. *Cosmic Consciousness*. New York: E.P. Dutton and Co., Inc., 1946.

Castaneda, C. *The Teachings of Don Juan*. New York: Ballantine Books, 1968.

Campbell, Joseph. *Myths to Live By*. New York: Bantam Books, 1970.

Carrel, Alexis. *Man the Unknown*. New York: Harper Brothers, 1955.

Chambers, John D., trans. *The Divine Pymander and Other Writings of Hermes Trismegistus*. New York: Samuel Weiser Inc., 1975.

Dee, Dr. John. *The Hieroglyphic Monad*. Translated by J.W. Hamilton-Jones. New York: Samuel Weiser Inc., 1975.

Dobin, Rabbi Joel C. *To Rule Both Day and Night: Astrology in the Bible, Midrash and Talmud*. New York: Inner Traditions International, 1977.

Eliade, Mircea. *Patterns in Comparative Religion*. Translated by Rosemary Sheed. New York: Meridian Books, 1958.

———. *The Sacred and the Profane*. Translated by Willard Trask. New York: Harcourt, Brace and World, 1959.

Epstein, Perle. *Kabbalah: The Way of the Jewish Mystic*. Garden City, New York: Doubleday and Co., Inc., 1978.

Fortune, Dion. *The Mystical Qabalah*. London: Ernest Benn, Ltd., 1970.

Franck, Adolphe. *The Kabbalah*. New Hyde Park, New York: University Books, 1967.

Franck, Frederick. *The Zen of Seeing*. New York: Vantage Press, 1973.

Gibran, Kahlil. *The Prophet*. New York: Alfred A. Knopf, 1964.

Ginzburg, Christian D. *The Essenes. The Kabbalah. Two Essays*. London: Routledge and Kegan Paul, Ltd., 1971.

Gray, William G. *The Ladder of Lights*. Toddington, Gt. Britain: Helios Book Service Ltd., 1968.

Halevi, Z'ev ben Shimon. *Adam and the Kabbalistic Tree*. New York: Samuel Weiser Inc., 1974.

_____. *An Introduction to the Cabala*. New York: Samuel Weiser Inc., 1972.

_____. *Kabbalah and Exodus*. Boulder, Colorado: Shambhala, 1980.

_____. *Kabbalah Tradition of Hidden Knowledge*. Farnborough, Hampshire, England: Thames & Hudson, 1979.

_____. *A Kabbalistic Universe*. New York: Samuel Weiser Inc., 1977.

_____. *The Way of the Kabbalah*. New York: Samuel Weiser Inc., 1976.

Hamilton, Edith. *The Ever Present Past*. New York: W. W. Norton, 1964.

Hixon, Lex. *Coming Home*. New York: Anchor Press, 1978.

Hoffman, Edward. *The Way of Splendor*. Boulder, CO: Shambhala, 1981.

James, William. *The Varieties of Religious Experience*. London/New York: Logmans Green and Co., 1941.

Jocelyn, John. *Meditations on the Signs of the Zodiac*. Spring Valley, NY: Rudolf Steiner Publications, 1970.

John of the Cross. *Dark Night of the Soul*. Translated by E. Allison Peers. New York: Image Books, 1959.

Jung, Jolanda. *The Psychology of C.G. Jung*. Translated by K.W. Bash. New Haven: Yale University Press, 1943.

Kaplan, Aryeh. *Meditation and the Bible*. New York: Samuel Weiser Inc., 1978.

Khan, Hazrat Inayat. *The Complete Sayings of Hazrat Inayat Khan*. New Lebanon, New York: Sufi Order Publications, 1978.

Khan, Pir Vilayat Inayat. *Sufi Masters*. The Sufi Order, 1971.

Krishnamurti, J. *The First and Last Freedom*. New York: Harper and Row, 1954.

Kushner, Lawrence. *The Book of Letters*. New York: Harper and Row, 1975.

Lao Tzu. *Tao Te Ching*. Translated by Ch'u Ta-Kao. New York: Samuel Weiser, 1973.

Leadbeater, C.W. *The Chakras*. Wheaton, Illinois: Theosophical Publishing House, 1969.

_____. *Man: Visible and Invisible*. Wheaton, Illinois: Theosophical Publishing House, 1969.

Love, Jeff. *The Quantum Gods*. Great Britain: Compton Russell Ltd., 1976.

Mathers, S.L. MacGregor. *The Kabbalah Unveiled*. New York: Samuel Weiser Inc., 1968.

Moore, Marcia and Mark Douglas. *Astrology: The Divine Science*. York Harbor, Maine: Arcane Publications, 1981.

d'Olivet, Fabre. *The Hebraic Tongue Restored*. Translated by Nayan Louise Redfield. New York: Samuel Weiser Inc., 1976.

Ouspensky, P.D. *The Symbolism of the Tarot*. Translated by A. Pogossky. New York: Dover Books, 1976.

Papus (Dr. Gérard Encausse). *The Qabala*. New York: Samuel Weiser Inc., 1977.

Poncé, Charles. *Kabbalah*. Wheaton, Illinois: Theosophical Publishing House, 1978.

Rumi, J. *Divani Shamsi Tabriz*. San Francisco: The Rainbow Bridge, 1973.

Schachter, Reb Zalman. *Fragments of a Future Scroll: Hassidim for the Aquarian Age.* Germantown, Pennsylvania: Leaves of Grass Press, 1975.

Scholem, Gershom. *Kabbalah.* New York: Quadrangle Books, The New York Times Book Company, 1974.

_____. *Major Trends in Jewish Mysticism.* New York: Schocken Books, 1973.

_____. *On the Kabbalah and Its Symbolism.* Translated by Ralph Manheim. New York: Schocken Books, 1973.

Schuré, Edouard. *The Great Initiates.* Translated by Gloria Rasberry. West Nyack, New York: St. George Books, 1961.

Schweitzer, Dr. Albert. *The Mystery of the Kingdom of God.* Translated by Walter Lowrie. New York: Schocken Books, 1970.

_____. *Pilgrimage to Humanity.* Translated by Walter E. Stuermann. New York: The Wisdom Library, 1961.

Smith, Huston. *The Religions of Man.* New York: Perennial Library, Harper & Row, Publishers, 1965.

_____. *Forgotten Truth.* New York: Harper Colophon Books, 1977.

Thompson, William Irwin. *At the Edge of History.* New York: Harper Colophon Books, 1971.

_____. *Passages About Earth.* New York: Harper and Row, 1973.

Three Initiates. *The Kybalion.* Chicago: The Yogi Publication Society Masonic Temple, 1936.

Waite, A.E. *The Holy Kabbalah.* New Hyde Park, New York: University Books, 1972.

Watts, A.W. *The Way of Zen.* New York: Vintage Books, 1957.

Weiner, Herbert. *Nine and One Half Mystics: The Kabbalah Today.* New York: Collier Books, 1969.

Westcott, W. Wynn. *Sepher Yetzirah: The Book of Formation*. New York: Samuel Weiser, Inc., 1971.

Wilhelm, Richard, and C. G. Jung. *The Secret of the Golden Flower*. London: Kegan Paul, Trench, Trubner and Co., Ltd., 1943.

For a comprehensive bibliography see also: Gershom G. Sholem, *Major Trends in Jewish Mysticism*, Schocken Books, New York, 1973.

Index

271

QUEST BOOKS
are published by
The Theosophical Society in America,
Wheaton, Illinois 60189–0270,
a branch of a world organization
dedicated to the promotion of the unity of
humanity and the encouragement of the study of
religion, philosophy, and science, to the end that
we may better understand ourselves and our place in
the universe. The Society stands for complete
freedom of individual search and belief.
In the Classics Series well-known
theosophical works are made
available in popular editions.
For more information
write or call.
1-708-668-1571

We publish books on:

Healing and Health • Metaphysics and Mysticism • Transpersonal Psychology Philosophy • Religion • Reincarnation, Science • Yoga and Meditation.

Other books of possible interest include:

The Cosmic Womb *by Arthur W. Osborn*
Our relationship with the infinite.

The Fire of Creation *by J. J. van der Leeuw*
The Holy Ghost and the universe as a dynamic process.

The Flame and the Light *by Hugh L'Anson Fausset*
Comparative study of Buddhism, Christianity and Vedas.

Judaism *by Jay G. Williams*
A history of the Jewish people and their religion.

Kabbalah *by Charles Ponce*
The history and doctrine of an ancient Jewish tradition.

Mystery Teachings in World Religions *by Florice Tanner*
Deep, hidden meanings behind tenets of major religions.

The Royal Road *by Stephan A. Hoeller*
The tarot and Kabbalah adapted for meditation purposes.

Transcendent Unity of Religions *by Frithjof Schuon*
A study of the exoteric and esoteric aspects of religion.

Whispers from the Other Shore *by Ravi Ravindra*
How religion can help us or hurt us in our seeking.

Yeshua Buddha *by Jay G. Williams*
New Testament theology as meaningful myth.

Available from:
The Theosophical Publishing House
P.O. Box 270, Wheaton, Illinois 60189-0270